Great Dialecticians
in Modern
Christian Thought

Great Dialecticians in Modern Christian Thought

ERNEST B. KOENKER

AUGSBURG PUBLISHING HOUSE
Minneapolis, Minnesota

GREAT DIALECTICIANS IN MODERN
CHRISTIAN THOUGHT

Library of Congress Catalog Card No. 76-135234

International Standard Book No. 0-8066-1115-4

Manufactured in the United States of America

CONTENTS

INTRODUCTION

We have set out to examine dialectic at work in a few outstanding Christian thinkers since the sixteenth century, as the chapter headings indicate. If one looks carefully at the operation of thought in each case he notes that it is this unexplored working of dialectic that provides the key to the deepest concern and methodology of each man. We wish to focus on types of dialectic, to see how opposition and reconciliation are dealt with in understanding man, his world, and his relation to God. Although we shall sketch the historical roots of dialectic we must restrict our consideration to select figures since the Reformation. We have not attempted to write a history of dialectical thinking, though our representative dialecticians summarize this history in a remarkable way. A good case could be made for the inclusion of other dialecticians, or for the substitution of more likely candidates than those chosen, but we may invoke the authority of Plato who argued that just as it is no disparagement to a hunter who, having found game in the wild wood, has not found all, so it may be no disparagement to our study if there are varieties of dialectical skill which have gone quite unnoticed.

In order to evaluate dialectic more exhaustively we should have to consider those intimations of opposition and unity expressed

by the poets, by Yeats and Robert Frost and Hölderlin. The poets have been most aware of the contradictory facets within the external world and in man's inner life. Rainer Maria Rilke saw them—and he was repulsed by the effort of reason to establish sharp oppositions in the world. The "hammers" and "teeth" of the following verse mirror the contradictions of reality:

> Between the hammers lives on the heart,
> As between the teeth the tongue,
> Which in spite of all
> Continues to praise.

The "heart" and a "worshiping tongue" celebrate a unity more fundamental for Rilke than the disunities of dialectic, of assertion and counter-assertion. It would also be revealing to explore the contributions of psychoanalytic theory and practice to the dialectic between psychic systems which takes place in psychic therapy. But all these types and operations of dialectic lie beyond our responsibility.

Coherence vs. Contradiction

There have always been those in the history of thought who have been anti-dialectical, who have emphasized ultimate coherence. Teilhard de Chardin, for example, could intuit Omega Point as the final convergence of evolutionary divergences. Teilhard's *gnosis* envisions a single evolutionary pattern ascending from inert matter to elementary life, from animal to man, from prehistory to the very present, and he extrapolates a similar "cosmogenesis" or "Christogenesis" leading to a "final crowning." Alfred North Whitehead, too, though he employs a profound duality between the primordial nature and consequent nature of God, yet sees reality in terms of a single creative process. The creative advance in the universe, while productive of genuine novelty and of the "many," is always the realization of a more complex unity. The fundamental thrust of his speculative philosophy is against all incoherences: they are brought together as partial and inconclusive aspects of a totality best described as an organism, structures of activity in an environment. In other words,

even those "sides" of God's nature which appear to stand in opposition to one another as static and as fluent are not dialectical oppositions for Whitehead but rather dual aspects of the single divine ordering. Here Whitehead resembles Chardin. Both dissolve possible oppositions into processes of dynamic achievement.

On the other hand, there have also always been the dialecticians, for whom tensions and contradictions have been more fundamental than unity. Life and history contain elements which shatter simple unities and all attempts of thought to establish harmony. Man experiences reality as diverse, as made up of elements which oppose one another. There may be some ultimate coherence, but what our dialecticians experience is a profound contrariness of things.

Some Sources of Dialectical Thinking

Dialectic is rooted in the many-faceted character of reality. Not only does our perception yield contradictory data. The real itself is complex. Ever and again thinkers have arisen to affirm opposition at the heart of reality itself. This opposition must—for true dialectic—be reconciled or overcome in some manner. Otherwise it would be simple polarity. Dialectic in this first sense arises from what the pre-Socratics already saw, from a deep-down contradiction in things.

But a second source becomes apparent as soon as one attempts to formulate "the truth" concerning reality in propositions. Dialecticians have engaged in the critical task of pointing to the relative character of truth. Truth must, somehow, be relative to my concrete, existential situation. I apprehend the truth from my limited perspective of time and place. Franz Kafka reflects this conflict between the one and many truths when he says, "It is difficult to state the truth, for it is, indeed, only one, but it is a living matter and has therefore a living, changing face." [1] Every statement of truth must be partial. It requires supplementation in the effort to attain a fuller truth by another, contradictory statement. Yet this statement, too, is partial. It requires harmonization, in some way, by a third. Whenever one's own subjective truth is set up as the single, entire truth the dialecticians have pointed to complementary or even contradictory ad-equations between the in-

tellect and reality. Plato contemplates a truth which might be one and the same for all men, but the dialogues witness the failure to encapsulate the truth in any abstract propositions. Seneca also has this second course in view when he speaks of dialectic being "divided into two parts, in words and things signified, i.e., in things spoken about and in words with which one speaks." [2] The distinction is reflected again by St. Bonaventure when he distinguishes carefully between truth a), as it exists unrevealed and eternal in the mind of God, and b) as perceived by me, but unexpressed, and truth c), as stated in simple or complex propositions. Truth as apprehended in man's seeing is participation in the divine light of the eternal order; as such it must be objective and changeless. Here is the deeper source of both a dialectical and anti-dialectical view of truth.

The situation is complicated, thirdly, when one moves from the truth as perceived by me to the truth of another distinct and irreplaceable *person.* Dialogue, as Martin Buber has demonstrated, gives rise to its own dialectic. And when one of the partners in this dialogue is the personal Creator-God, another form of dialectic is evident. Dialectic may be employed in many fields, but the *logos* about *theos,* theology, is bound to be dialectical—though the particular grounds for this dialectical character, as illustrated by our representative dialecticians, may become the battle-ground for theologians.

But these "sources" of dialectic have a deeper source still, pointed to by Heraclitus and Plato and Hegel, the law of dialectical polarity-and-unity, according to which ultimate contraries and thus also contradictions are correlatives of one another. They are related to one another as distinct aspects of a single whole. The final coherence of opposites may be hidden to man, the opposites may be reconciled only in the divine activity. Still, by the very nature of dialectic, such oppositions are finally related to one another in some "higher" unity.

Where do our master-dialecticians discern such unity in the face of the deep-down cleavages in reality? We should be ready to accept in the case of certain dialecticians, at least, only the faint premonition of ultimate unity. They live under the continual, agonizing threat of awesome disunities. Their lives and thought,

as in the case of Luther, a Kierkegaard, an Elert, reflect the aweful tensions and disharmonies of a divided self. Yet even here we should be careful to avoid reading the fearful hammers of contradiction, under which they suffered and struggled, as exclusive and final. The tenuous thread of Christian faith was still sufficient to reconcile the oppositions, to give a confident answer to the clamant counter-voices. They lived in the sure hope of final reconciliation, but they had not grasped it, nor could they hope ever to grasp it with their finite minds. A more tangible synthesis may be anticipated from others among our dialecticians, a resolution attainable by man's rational faculties, some reconciliation forming a present possession.

We shall wish to ask, therefore, whether the particular dialectic under consideration is a pistic dialectic, i.e., determined by and residing in faith, or a gnostic dialectic, formed by and finding resolution in knowledge.[3] A kind of Faustian thirst to push knowledge beyond its human limits seems to drive the dialectician, so that he would establish himself in some Satanic pact which promises to transcend the contradictory "Yes" and "No" of jurisprudence, medicine, philosophy, and theology, too. Does the dialectician under consideration seek to gain a perspective beyond faith or "above" faith in order to judge reality?

It would be too much to expect all dialectic to operate in a uniform manner. Still all pursue their theological task from the basic perspective of an open dialogue. All, moreover, affirm opposition at the heart of life and thought. In these minimal but essential senses the men are dialectical thinkers. We shall have occasion to note an "antithetic" type, for whom the contradictions stand out in their awesome extremes, and a "synthetic" type, where the contradictions are reconciled in some "higher" synthesis. But by the very nature of the oppositions and the theological quest itself both types drive forward to a mediation of contradictions which renders their provisional, preliminary differences of type only alternative modes of achieving final reconciliation.

For each of our dialecticians the oppositions are located quite differently, are mediated quite differently, and quite different goals are set for the entire process of reconciliation. Dialectical thinking follows quite different courses, and we should be ready to note di-

vergences within each type which are as essential as their similarities. Tillich's dialectic of correlation, for example, becomes a highly individual and distinctive method, with intimate links to the content of his entire system. Bultmann's existential dialectic presupposes a very specific understanding of Heidegger's analysis of man as well as a very technical understanding of the New Testament. We will, therefore, have to suggest a contextual approach to the operations of dialectic, interpreting each operation in the context of the specific problems and resources available to each thinker. Structural similarities there will be, but our concern for unity should not be permitted to blur the highly individualistic features of each man's discourse.

The Opponents of Dialectic

There have always been those who, like Tertullian, have opposed "all attempts to produce a mottled Christianity of Stoic, Platonic and dialectic composition. We want no curious disputation after possessing Christ Jesus. . . ." [4] For Tertullian dialectic was simply the equivalent of uncertainty, changeability, and inconclusiveness. With characteristic insight, which presaged the course of dialectical dissolutions in the course of Christian history, he saw dangerous relativizing of the one, sure, undialectical truth of Christianity. Christian faith is "having the truth." Dialectic, with its ever-critical negations and modifications, is always "seeking the truth." [5] It is always finding contradictions of one kind or another in simple assertions of truth, always merely approximating the truth. One does not progressively search for new knowledge when one possesses knowledge in Jesus Christ. In this sense—a respectable meaning of the term—Tertullian was a dogmatist in opposition to all dialecticians. Underlying his opposition was a different theory of truth, the view that one must know absolutely if he can know at all, in contrast to the view that sees knowledge as always relative to circumstances.

For Tertullian Jesus is one, clear, unchanging message from God, not some two-fold message which is again in danger of becoming threefold or fourfold. The certainty of Tertullian's faith also gave him security of life, singleness of purpose, and an unambiguous

morality. Tertullian's suspicions of a relativistic, hydra-headed dialectic break forth from time to time in the Medieval and modern Christian tradition, e.g., in St. Bernard's denunciation of Abelard's dialectic and in the unknown author of *The Imitation of Christ,* who advocates a settled faith in Christ in the face of excessive theological subtleties. The dialecticians have always dissolved fixations of doctrine: with their contradictions and insistence on dialogue they have introduced movement into thought, a movement which spurns provisional resting places and launches forth into the uncertainties of an endless quest.

Some Questions to Be Considered

We must consider among our dialecticians who follow whether their dialectic is provisional or sustained. Is dialectic seen as merely a superficial or relative feature of thought or reality? As Jacob Taubes observes, dialectic "is not a coach that can be stopped at will." [6] Is its *locus* the inner soul of man or is it seen as operative in history? Are the dialectical oppositions seen as complementary elements in a unified whole, like the negative, female principle, *yin* and the positive, male principle, *yang* of Chinese philosophy? Is the dialectic essentially a means of resolving contradictions by means of a reconciling principle, so that a single, supreme principle emerges "beyond," or "through," the dialectical oppositions? This harmonization appears already at the birth of dialectic. Heraclitus objected to those who failed to see unity in opposition, "They do not understand how that which differs with itself is in agreement: harmony consists of opposing tension, like that of the bow and the lyre." [7]

Greek and Hebrew Dialectic

In fact, one may claim that the metaphysician's ascent from the relative to the absolute and the theologian's positing of the sacred, or holy, in relation to the non-sacred are both dialectical operations. They involve opposition to existing things, but are still based on the participation of those things in the absolute or the sacred. At the beginning of Greek speculation Anaximander of Miletus (*fl. c.* 560) posited the *apeiron* (τὸ ἄπειρον), the Boundless or Limitless,

over against the things that are (τὰ ὄντα). The *apeiron* is itself the unoriginated source, the ἀρχή, of all that is—eternal, indestructible, divine. Though itself free from opposition, the *apeiron* is the font and terminus of oppositions which pervade existing things. If it is clear that we cannot construct a theory of dialectic from the minimal fragments of Anaximander it is equally clear that a dialectical interpretation, daring but quite undeveloped, informed Anaximander's positing of the *apeiron*.

Our dialecticians find different oppositions in the Biblical sources, as, e.g., between appearance and reality in the struggle for faith (cf. 2 Cor. 6, 9-10), between the divine Yes and No (2 Cor. 1, 17 ff.), between God as Redeemer and as Enemy (Isaiah 63, 7-16). The Hebrews did not analyze the modes of opposition in Jahweh's relations to the world, the tensions, polarities, and discontinuities between Creator and creatures, which the prophets were to underscore with their symbolic acts. Jahweh is to be identified neither with the creative powers of nature nor with the purely transcendent. He is both active in nature and distinct from all particular phenomena. The biblical view illumines both the strange reality of God and the familiar objects of sense: the things of this world are seen in a new dimension when viewed as elements in God's world, but God, too, discloses himself only in and through the realities of this world.

So a true dialectic between their source and the things that are pulses through the very earliest history of dialectic. Greek and Hebrew strands were to be intertwined in complex ways, but always the dialecticians did the intertwining, or they protested the intertwining, so that the course of Western Christian thought has been the story of dialectical unions and dissolutions.

Notes

1. Quoted by Hannah Arendt, "Understanding and Politics," *The Partisan Review,* 20 (1953), p. 377.
2. Epist. I, 1.
3. Cf. Jacob Taubes, "Philosophers Speak of God: A Review Article," *The Journal of Religion,* XXXIV (April, 1954), 120-26.
4. *De Praescriptione,* vii.

5. Tertullian could point to considerable evidence of attenuation in thought. Cicero comments on the skeptical outcome of the New Academy; of Plato's books he says that nothing is affirmed with certainty, though every thing is argued *"in utramque partem"* (both *pro* and *contra.*). Cicero, *Academica,* I, xii, 46.
6. "On the Nature of the Theological Method: Some Reflections on the Methodological Principles of Tillich's Theology," *The Journal of Religion,* vol. XXXIV (1954), p. 17.
7. Frag. 51. Kathleen Freeman, *Ancilla to the Pre-Socratics Philosophers* (Cambridge, Mass.: Harvard University Press, 1957), p. 28.

1

ANCIENT AND MEDIEVAL DIALECTICIANS: THE LENGTHENING SHADOW OF PLATO

One's view of the origin of dialectic will differ according to whether he considers the Platonic question-and-answer method essential or accepts certain views regarding identity and contradiction as distinguishing features of dialectical thinking. When Anaximander posited his *apeiron,* the Boundless, as source and goal of all the oppositions in existing things he demonstrated that he was, in this second view, a dialectician of creative, primal power. Yet it is Heraclitus of Ephesus (*fl. c.* 500) who stands at the fountainhead of Western dialectic. He made dialectic the principle of mediation between oppositions in both the logical and real worlds. His *logos* comprehends in a dynamic unity the warring disunities of discourse and life. He was fascinated by a *Realdialektik* running through all things, a thought that was to call forth the admiration of Hegel. [1]

Heraclitus' Contradiction and Change

Already in Heraclitus' sophisticated dialectic there is an ontological "turning" of contradictions into their opposites, "And what is in us is the same thing: living and dead, awake and sleeping, as well as young and old; for the latter (of each pair of opposites)

having changed becomes the former, and this again having changed becomes the latter." [2] It is not surprising that Heraclitus was misunderstood as denying the principle of contradiction when he asserted that "we are and we are not." [3]

Heraclitus saw change as the fiery crucible in which polar opposites interact to form new harmony: "That which is in opposition is in concert, and from things that differ comes the most beautiful harmony." [4] It is the task and power of the fiery, divine *logos* to order the pluralities of strife. Opposites are never independent of one another. They require each other. Discord is always the condition for harmony. Ultimate reality, or "God", is not independent of tension; He is "completed" by cosmic strife: "God is day-night, winter-summer, war-peace, satiety-famine." [5]

Actually, Heraclitus must share his distinction as innovator with a contemporary, Parmenides (*fl. c.* 475), a citizen of Elea in Southern Italy, who rivals him in every respect. Both Heraclitus and Parmenides were keenly aware of the demand to mediate the oppositions in life. Their similarities outweigh their profound differences. They were to earn the distinction from Heidegger of being "the two decisive thinkers." [6]

Parmenides' Identity and the Changeless

It is not surprising that Heraclitus elicited the violent contradictions of the Eleatics. In place of Heraclitean contradiction and change, Parmenides puts identity and the changeless. As sharpest critic of Heraclitus' "two-headed" doctrine, he gave classic expression to the absolute logical contradiction between being and not being. Only Being is. Correspondingly, "nothing" cannot also "be." It must by formal logic be excluded from Being. Being (ὄν) is distinct from the multitude of existing beings (ὄντα). Being is motionless, void of becoming, without beginning or end, always identical with itself. [7] No one has read the evidences of alteration and decay so consistently in terms of an absolute monism of Being. So in the thought of both Heraclitus and Parmenides a mediation of opposites occurs. If the mediating principle is Becoming for Heraclitus and Being for Parmenides the method by which they arrive at this primordial unity is the harmonization of opposites.

They testify to the dialectical power that distinguishes the very beginning of Greek reflective thinking.

Origins in Pre-Socratics or in Plato?

On the question of the origin of dialectic one must give due weight to a basic statement from Aristotle. He says even of the late period of Socrates' activity, "there was as yet none of the dialectical power which enables people even without knowledge of the essence to speculate about contraries and inquire whether the same science deals with contraries." [8] The rise of this power, Aristotle indicates, is to be associated only with Plato, and not with Socrates. Here in the *Metaphysics* we have a clear, explicit judgment regarding the origin of the dialectical method. [9] Yet according to the record of Diogenes Laertius, Aristotle credits Zeno with being the "inventor of dialectic." [10] How is one to clarify this apparent discrepancy in Aristotle? Evidently two distinct meanings of the term are involved: the dialectic of Zeno is quite different from that of Plato. Zeno refutes the view of his opponents, that things are many, by deducing impossible consequences from it. He establishes his own positive position on the unity and indivisibility of being by demonstrating the contradictory conclusions to which his opponent's view leads: "If things are many, they must be both small and great: so small as to have no size, so large as to be infinite." [11] It is interesting to note that these very contradictory conclusions of Zeno were later to be affirmed, in their dialectical extremes, as the *deux infinis* of Pascal.

In a similar way, Zeno argues against the possibility of motion by pointing out that it involves contradiction ,"That which moves, moves neither in the place in which it is, nor in that in which it is not." [12] This reduction of an opponent's view to absurdity through demonstrating contradictory consequences can be understood, according to Aristotle's judgement cited by Diogenes Laertius, as a form of dialectic. The principles of identity and contradiction are seen as aspects of reality. Plato, too, was to refute untenable views by demonstrating their contradictory character. But there is no evidence that the conversational procedure was integral to Zeno's method. Robinson concludes, therefore, that dialectic did not begin with Zeno, for "whereas Plato and Aristotle both considered

question-and-answer essential to dialectic, Zeno probably never entertained the idea that question-and-answer was necessary to good method." [13]

Plato the Supreme Dialectician

We prefer to recognize in the contradictions of Heraclitus, Parmenides, and Zeno actual forms of dialectic. Still it is clearly the genius of Plato that dominates the beginnings. Though dialectic did not begin as his creation no one practiced it with more consummate skill. Dialogue here reaches its high point in the movement of disclosing truth; it is the cardinal factor in Plato's method. Basically it is a means of examining and criticizing ideas. It is a quest for knowledge and the criticism of this quest. Participants in the dialogues are forced to admit that they do not know something of which they previously had claimed certain knowledge. Plato's dialectical skill accounts for both the penetration of his argument and the comprehensiveness of his analysis of being and becoming, the one and many. Already in Plato dialectic faces the clear and present danger of lapsing into sophistry or rhetoric. In the figure of Protagoras dialectic gives way to rhetoric: the educated man knows how to use the power of words in the art of persuasion. Protagoras is a leading sophist because full responsibility breaks down in the quest for truth: he is satisfied with semblances of truth rather than with the pursuit of analysis through such semblances. Plato, however, insists on pushing inquiry beyond semblances to precise concepts and integral judgments. In his hands dialectic illuminates all that is.

In its initial and simplest sense in Plato dialectic stands for dialogue, deriving from διαλέγεσθαι "to converse with someone." In this sense the term need carry no distinct philosophical overtones: the philosopher will on occasion converse about things at his feet or before his eyes. [14] It may be commonplace discourse about commonplace topics or things. But knowledge of one sort or another is professed or presumed: an interlocutor in one of the dialogues may show that even here a hidden knowledge or a profound lack of knowledge is at issue. Refutations fairly flourish on exposing the superficiality of definitions. Contradictions emerge which cry out for correction. They force the dynamic movement of

thinking and answering that is the soul of dialectic. At times the contradictions are as sharp as Zeno's. For opposition sparks the dialectical examination. It is necessary in order to know anything. One understands some quality or phenomenon fully only through confronting, actually incorporating into oneself the opposing quality, as courage absorbs fear.[15]

If the dialoguers progress from the limited point of view represented by each participant and agree upon a third point of view, which in some way includes the earlier alternatives or oppositions, and if this new perspective is again met and comprehended in a higher harmony (συμφονεῖν), then, if the process is pursued far enough and faithfully enough, it will bring the participants from becoming to being, two cognitively different realms rather than two distinct realms of being. It is no overwhelming problem that the dialogues break off either because of some other engagement or the exhaustion of the participants' mental resources. In the very nature of the case such a quest for knowledge and such criticism of the quest can and must be engaged in with other interlocutors at other banquets, or on other streets. Through dialogue the purely subjective characteristics of views are expunged. One explores, in marvelous freedom, possibilities. One wins his way to more adequate conceptions. Each view is the alternative of a specific person; so an interaction takes place which illuminates the person and allows the views of each person to complement, to contribute to the truth of another. But the process itself never ends.

The Royal Science

In contrast to the restricted sciences of hunting or governing, dialectic is the royal science ἡ βασιλική τέχνη.[16] It aims at the ultimate unity of all the sciences. It is not limited, like the particular sciences, to specific aspects or kinds of being. It embraces all of the "beings" in its quest for knowledge of being. This is why dialectic is also "the coping stone of the sciences."[17] Knowledge cannot go beyond dialectic; for this reason it is the ultimate subject in the course of studies pursued by the philosopher kings. It is not begun before the age of thirty—only after mathematics and astronomy have been mastered, i.e., only after the most concen-

trated mental disciplines. So dialectic is a propaedeutic to the exercise of freedom on the part of the good man and the qualified ruler. It must lead, as fundamental knowledge, to the transformation of the possessor, for such knowledge is not distinct from the reality of the thinker.

Plato employs both an ascending and a descending dialectic. The ascending dialectic is a quest for knowledge through a process of inquiry. It climbs from unexamined opinions to first principles. Usually it begins with the preliminary quest for a definition, e.g., of justice, or knowledge, or courage. The *Republic* follows such an ascending dialectic, moving from becoming to being. The descending dialectic is a process of demonstration: it examines the consequences of something that has already been attained. The sensible world is explained in terms of ideas, or the ideal is used to evaluate the actual as, e.g., in the *Timaeus,* where the movement is from being to becoming. Yet both ascending and descending dialectic are to be understood as "becoming:" the ontological situation is always viewed in terms of thoughts and the words which express these thoughts. Being, a state of stability and certainty, is the ideal culmination of a dialectical inquiry, but the inquiry is still conducted in the chaotic state of "becoming." If one were to go far enough in such inquiry he would arrive at being—understood, however, in terms of the dialectical process itself, and not as some static realm beyond the objects of sense. Becoming and perishing lie between that which has being and that which has not: being and non-being mutually require one another. [18] Non-being also *"is"* in a certain sense—a sense to be explored in the modern age by Boehme, Hegel, Tillich, and Heidegger. We must, however, be aware that Plato's own epistemological concerns are often ignored and are viewed exclusively as ontological concerns. His whole contextual approach to being, becoming, and non-being very early came to be subverted.

Becoming and Being, Opinion and Knowledge

Correlative with "becoming" is "opinion," the uncritical acceptance of what is given, the experienced, the "sensible." "Being," on the other hand, is correlated with "knowledge," a grasp of the

first principles from which all knowing proceeds, the "intelligible." Opinion (δόξα), which is engrossed in the "many," gives way in the course of the dialectical process to "knowledge" of the "idea," i.e., of both "what is" and "what is known." One moves from a state of opinion and changeability to a state of stability. Through dialectic one wins his way to more adequate conceptions; dialectic spans the reaches from the confusions of sense perceptions to the steady gaze of eternal ideas. [19]

In the *Republic* Plato works his way up the ladder of the double-divided line, yet Socrates never professes to be on the fourth level of the line, the level of science, ἐπιστήμη. He is not simply speaking ironically when he denies such science. He is still on the third level, the level of arts. He never claims the ideal of having arrived at science; he has not run the gauntlet of all objections. Still he holds converse with the divine order, which is the structure of the thing known. [20] The knower takes into himself what he knows. Any attempt to formulate "Platonic doctrines" overlooks this coalescence of knower and known, of epistemology and ontology in Plato. The structure of things and the structure of the mind are ultimately equated. Thus there is in Plato the encompassing unity of thought, which binds together the dialectical relations of knowledge and the universe.

For Plato the dialectical method *is* the scientific method: *only* the dialectical procedure can effectively free one from images or shadows, on the first level, and sensible objects, the original of these shadows, on the second, and hypotheses, on the third; it alone can bring one to the "ideas," the originals of the hypotheses. Its aim is, finally, to "see" the Good itself. Only this procedure will bring one to science itself (ἐπιστήμη). It alone yields a "synoptic view of all reality." [21] Its aim is to reach an ultimate unity of all the sciences, to discover their necessary inter-connections, rather than remain with the plurality of sciences represented by the unrelated hypotheses on the third level.

Aristotle and Plotinus

In place of the dialectical method which in Plato leads ultimately to a single science, at the top level of the divided line, one meets

in Aristotle various methods, among which is the dialectical, and a number of sciences dealing with different subject matters, employing distinct methods, and aiming at specific purposes. He wishes to tighten up the rather loose dialectical process in Plato. Aristotle states the necessity for pursuing an investigation by way of dialectic, "because the ability to raise searching difficulties on both sides of a subject will make us detect more easily the truth and error about the several points that arise." [22] He employs this method himself in the science of metaphysics. Dialectic, as illustrated there, examines opinions that are "generally accepted" in order to get at the basic principles underlying things. It engages in criticism in order to uncover "the principles of all inquiries." [23] Such a first principle will "command belief in and by itself." [24] The most certain of such principles is the principle of contradiction: "the same attribute cannot at the same time belong and not belong to the same subject and in the same respect." [25] If one were to abrogate this principle, Aristotle says, every discourse would dissolve its own conditions, and so all discourse would be dissolved. When one speaks of a "dialectical reconciliation of opposites" one can only have in mind the Socratic operation of criticizing concepts and discovering a higher generic concept to comprehend the oppositions. [26]

But Aristotle sees dialectic as the art of testing or examining those things for which philosophy is the art of knowledge [27] It works from premises which are probable in the eyes of reasonable men. It can be no more than a critical process prior to philosophy, properly speaking. Aristotle wishes—in contrast to the one science of Plato—to establish a strictly scientific knowledge, one which demonstrates by syllogistic reasoning the necessary conclusions which follow for each kind of subject matter when one starts with first principles that are self-evidently true. Sophistry he distinguishes from both dialectic and philosophy because "sophistic is Wisdom which exists only in semblance." [28] Sophistry works from premises which merely *seem* to be probable.

Plotinus broke with the intimate unity of epistemology and ontology in Plato to create from Plato's dialectic of discovery a mystical and otherworldly religious philosophy. His dialectic is a saving intellectual activity by which the indivdual soul sloughs

off images of the material world. Dialectic is one of the ways by which the soul reascends from "here" to "there" until it is reunited with the intelligible world of Mind. The soul is lifted by knowledge of Being: through an ethical life and the dialectical ascent it is progressively purified. Dialectic is "the most precious part of philosophy." [29] It yields intimate and comprehensive knowledge of the structure of that higher world of Mind in which the individual soul participates; through contemplation the soul returns to Mind from which it was estranged. [30]

St. Augustine's Dialectic of Creator and Creature

In St. Augustine we meet that limitless reflection which was to be so profoundly suggestive for over a thousand years. There is not one dialectic operative here but many: he passes through several stages. In the *De Ordine* St. Augustine gives the exalted neo-Platonic definition of dialectic as "the science of sciences which teaches men both how to teach and how to learn." [31] But he employs the term himself more narrowly to describe "the science of reasoning." [32] It is equivalent to logic, and this equivalency of the two terms pervades Medieval usage. It "deals with inferences, and definitions, and divisions." [33] Along with grammar and rhetoric, dialectic (logic) stands among the liberal arts, the "trivium."

There is also the neo-Platonic-mystical dialectic of alienation from God and return to the divine. Still in place of the Plotinian efflux and influx St. Augustine acknowledges the Biblical Creator and creature; there are creatures which are in danger of lapsing again into nothing. The split between creation and Creator was to be widened by Luther and Pascal, and extended further by Kierkegaard and Barth. Augustine refers again and again to this dialectic of Creator and creatures, as, e.g., in the restlessness of the human heart created for repose in God, or in the chorus of all created things:

> I asked the earth, and it answered me "I am not he"; and whatsoever are in it confessed the same. I asked the sea and the deeps, and the living creeping things, and they answered, "We are not thy God, seek above us." I asked the moving air; and the whole air with his inhabitants answered, "Anaxi-

> menes was deceived, I am not God." I asked the heavens, sun, moon, stars, "Nor," say they, "are we the God whom thou seekest." And I replied unto all the things which encompass the door of my flesh, "Ye have told me of my God, that ye are not He; tell me something of Him." And they cried out with a loud voice, "He made us." [34]

Man recognizes in himself contingent and imperfect being. In this very awareness there is also present to man's consciousness, undemonstrated and beyond all demonstration, the awareness of the unconditioned divine Source. This God, so utterly superior to the highest creature, is not to be found other than in man's inmost soul: "I looked for you everywhere, my God, but when I found you, you were within me." [35] This is the intimate wisdom *(intima scientia)* of God that is as close to the soul as the consciousness of its own existing, knowing, and willing. [36] The perfections of the created order abound in a pre-eminent manner in God; perfections that we love and desire in the creatures are actually the perfections that belong in a total and self-sufficient manner to God alone. Man is not a divine being, as he is for Plato and Plotinus. There is no scintilla of the divine essence in him to support such a claim. He is created and thus contingent being. He is not a part of the divine order. Yet paradoxically this same creature participates in and steadily reflects an order that is eternal and divine. All that has being radiates a splendor that belongs to God, its Source.

St. Augustine sees this reflected most clearly in the divine truth which man shares. Man is capable of knowing the immutable, the immaterial, the intelligible, through the light of a self-subsisting truth, a unique "sun," the light of God within him. He uses arguments learned from the Platonists to refute the sceptics' denial of a truth from which they felt excluded: these very sceptics must participate in a truth which they strive to attain in an absolute form. Truth, which most certainly dwells in the soul which is seeking after the truth, transcends every finite expression; it requires an unconditioned norm and Source, the True-itself. [37] Augustine uses the broad Platonic dialectic to establish the truths of Aristotelian logic, i.e., of dialectic in the narrower sense. He says of the logical foundations of knowledge, "Through dialectic I have learned that these and many other things—which it would be

very tedious to enumerate—are true, true in themselves, howsoever our senses may be affected. [38]

Although we have emphasized the Platonic framework of St. Augustine's dialectic there can be no question but that the key truth not found among the Platonists, that the very *logos* became man in Christ, deepened and expanded his dialectic. The all-present God domiciles with man in the Incarnation and in his Mystical Body, the Church. He was to expand the dialectic of union of God and man in Christ to a Trinitarian dialectic of unity of Father and Son in the gift of the Spirit. His Trinitarian thinking enjoys the confidence that philosophical reason will confirm the mystery of faith. This is why he finds images of the Trinity everywhere in the created order; the self is especially conscious of the triad of being, knowing, and purposing. [39]

One might explore a dialectic of nature and grace, or the letter and the spirit in St. Augustine, but all the cleavages present in the universe are harmonized in an hierarchical order, extending from the lowest to the highest. Every element in the divinely-ordained unity of being has its own distinctive purpose and strives to fulfill its end by accomplishing this purpose. Love is the comprehensive principle that binds all the scattered elements of the universe into a unity, as one sees this reflected later in the theology of love in St. Bonaventure and in Dante.

Medieval and Renaissance Dialecticians

It is the gnostic theology of Pseudo-Dionysius (fifth century) and John Scotus Erigena (*c.* 800—880) that informs the dialectical theology of the late Middle Ages and the Renaissance. It is remarkable to note how much of the later development is present in these neo-Platonic masters. They are the matrix of Meister Eckhart's (*c.* 1260-1327) distinction between "natured Nature," the divine revealed in personal form, and "non-natured Nature," the unoriginated reality which is unrevealed and utterly beyond human knowledge. Cusanus and Bruno and Spinoza's "natura naturans" and "natura naturata" are foreshadowed here. In his treatise *On the Divine Names* Pseudo-Dionysius asserts that the Divine Being comprehends and yet transcends all contraries. This

super-essential Deity is inaccessible and incomprehensible to human reason: no predicates or attributes can express His Being. [40] He is pure Being and yet no being, called by every name as related to differentiated being, and yet as Ultimate Godhead, the Nameless.

Erigena follows Dionysius in distinguishing between two ways of approaching God, the affirmative and negative way (καταφατική και ἀποφατική). All names apply to God only metaphorically, since God is super-essential Essence, infinitely transcending the content of all names man may apply to him. He is beyond all oppositions, which necessarily characterize human thought; he is the reconciliation of contraries, [41] the unity of both positive and negative. [42] Erigena deepens the dialectic of Plotinus, St. Augustine, Proclus, and Pseudo-Dionysius: he finds it cut into Nature, i.e., the totality of things, including *ea quae sunt, et ea quae non sunt.* The nothing out of which God created all is not privation of being but negation of being within God. [43] The created order is the theophany of God. Erigena's fourfold division of Nature reveals the dialectical structure of reality:

> Nature which creates and is not created,
> Nature which is created and creates,
> Nature which is created and does not create, and
> Nature which neither creates nor is created. [44]

Peter Abelard (1079-1142), the brilliant dialectician of the hill of St. Genevieve, was seen by his contemporaries as a dangerous innovator. He intruded logic into matters of faith. Christian doctrine he saw at once rational and logical. [45] Though truth must be single, unambiguous, and certain still the faith "handed down" via the traditions is often received in an ambiguous and even contradictory form. In the *Sic et Non* he organizes opposing statements from Scripture and the Fathers on a host of subjects—no less than 168 subjects. He confronts these opposing assertions with one another. He does this not to harmonize them but so that "young readers might be provoked to the greatest exertion in the quest for truth and through such exertion sharpen their faculties." [46] For it is "through doubting that we come to inquire, and through inquiry we perceive the truth." [47] Theology cannot avoid the dialectical task of eliminating false arguments. For

dialectic is the art of distinguishing between arguments that are valid and invalid. [48] Without dialectic it is impossible for faith to defend itself against the sophistical reasoning of the heretics. [49]

It is clear that Abelard approached the contradictory statements from Scripture and the Fathers as seeming contradictions. He gives examples, in the Prologue, of how some of them may be harmonized. He is bold in setting forth their dangerous, contrary affirmations, yet the *gesta dei* to which they refer are one and incontrovertible. The method of inquiry practiced so effectively by Abelard was to be transformed by the great Scholastics who followed into the harmonizing of the traditions.

St. Thomas Aquinas (1225-74) had appropriated the Aristotelian scale of nature stretching from dead matter, through plants, lower animals, higher animals, and man. Thomas extended the levels of this hierarchy of being from all contingent beings to the necessary being, God. The basic tension between contingency and necessity underlies his proofs for the existence of God. Still the tension does not constitute contradiction: contingent being simply requires as its cause necessary being. St. Thomas, in affirming the *analogia entis,* was rejecting the dialectical way, which destroys unity and proportionality and denies similarities of relation. In the *analogia entis,* which presupposes an hierarchical order of being, there are, indeed, tensions. But harmony and proportionality between the disparate elements effectively rules out contradictions. There are apparent opposites, such as law and grace, nature and the supernatural, Creator and creature. These appear to be set over against each other, but in reality they are structured in a comprehensive, complementary unity, a unity in which the cosmos "below" corresponds to the heavens "above," where all created things reflect their prototypes, the *Urbilder,* where human reason mirrors the order of divine reason because man was created in the image of God. [50]

Thus there is commensurability between the finite order and the infinite order: the perfections of creatures are found in the Creator in a super-eminent way, compatible with God's infinity. St. Thomas' treatment of analogy by no means led him to assert that "God is" in the same sense *(univoce)* that "the world is." Between the being of the Creator and the being of the created world he recognizes

an *infinite* difference of being. Only God "is" in the primary, complete sense of the word. When one says the world "is," another sense, qualified and derivative, is to be understood. So the being of the world is to be understood by analogy to the being of God. The term "being" is no mere empty name, but in both instances a hidden reality, being itself, is affirmed. [51]

Quite different forces had arisen to animate the thinking of Cardinal Nicholas of Cusa (1401-64). Nicholas held that one can never reach the infinite by taking measurements in the finite world. On this St. Thomas would have agreed. But Thomas did not see God as the *coincidentia oppositorum,* the synthesis and unity of the opposites found in the pluralities of finite reality. Thomas could not, like Nicholas, detect a positive and negative aspect in everything. Cusanus shatters the shell of the limited Medieval universe and leaves it interminate and indetermined: though the universe is not declared to be positively "infinite" still no *"terminae"* are set to its reaches and no precise determinations are to be set to our knowledge of it. [52] The world for Cusanus is still finite, but God is infinite. There is simply no proportion between finite and infinite. God is the eternal living unity of all the pluralities in the world, read by Cusanus as opposites. In God, the unity of all opposites, every possibility and distinction and contradiction coheres in a boundless unity. Every entity is infinitely near and infinitely far from the divine. Everything in the universe has divine significance; nothing is divine, because it "comes short" of the divine.

Thus man's knowledge, too, is infinitely near to and infinitely far from reality. The more fully we realize our inability to know the full truth about anything the closer to the truth we will be. We will have learned the lesson of "informed ignorance," the *docta ignorantia.* [53] When we come to realize the incomprehensible character of things we will be drawing near the truth. [54] Our knowledge cannot be precise, nor can we know the essence of material beings. Even man's knowledge of creatures is only approximate and conjectural: finite things are known only in their relation to or in comparison with other things. But we cannot comprehend God, who is both greatest being *(maximum)* in which all things inhere, and least being *(minimum),* which cannot be

less than it is.[55] He is the absolute coincidence of opposites, *absoluta coincidentia oppositorum.*[56]

The thought of Cusanus was developed further by Giordano Bruno (1548-1600), who brought Renaissance philosophy to imaginative expression. Bruno expanded the Copernican universe and brought the new astronomy to bear on Cusanus' reflections: the universe is not only limitless but infinite in space.[57] There is an infinity of unending universes in limitless space. Solar systems rise and decay. No one star or planet can be called the "navel center" among these countless worlds. The beginning and end of this process, limitless in time and space, are to be found in the monads, the basic units of change, which are endowed with perception and appetite.

Bruno's dialectic of the infinite and finite appears again unmistakeably in Spinoza and in Leibnitz. Spinoza must engage in a dialectic between "Nature" and "God" before settling upon their pantheistic resolution in identity, his *"Deus sive Natura."* But for speculative originality no one in the modern period was to outdo Bruno's conception of the identity of subject and object, the coincidence of all contraries in a single infinite continuum. In his universes, "contraries are within contraries, wherefore it is not difficult to compass the knowledge that each thing is within each other . . . ."[58]

Dialectical thinking can claim distinguished ancient and medieval genealogy. But modern thought has been forced to face still more uncompromising polarities. The extremes in the inner self and in the external world have widened since the Renaissance to reveal new and deepened chasms. Our "moderns," to whom we now turn, have added new circles to the depths of Medieval infernos. Each has been forced to face new cleavages in a broken world. Each has shared the horrors of Dante when forsaken by Vergil:[59]

> So the sweet Guide and Father leaves me here,
> and I stay on in doubt with yes and no
> dividing all my heart to hope and fear.

Notes

1. *Lectures on the History of Philosophy* (London: Kegan Paul, Trench, Trübner & Co., 1892), vol. I, 278 ff.
2. Fr. 88. Kathleen Freeman, *Ancilla to the Pre-Socratic Philosophers,* p. 25.
3. Fr. 49a; p. 28.
4. Fr. 8; p. 25.
5. Fr. 67; p. 29.
6. *Einführung in die Metaphysik* (Max Niemeyer, Tübingen, 1953), p. 96. We follow Heidegger in his emphasis on similarity rather than disagreement between Heraclitus and Parmenides. Cf. *op. cit.,* p. 74.
7. Fr. 78; pp. 43-4.
8. M 4, 1078b25. Richard McKeon, *The Basic Works of Artistotle* (New York: Random House, 1941), p. 894.
9. Cf. Richard Robinson, *Plato's Earlier Dialectic* (Oxford: Clarendon Press, 1953), pp. 88-92.
10. Εὐερετῆς διαλεκτικῆς, *Lives* IX 25. Cf. VIII 57.
11. Fr. 1; p. 47.
12. Fr. 4; p. 47.
13. *Op. cit.,* p. 91.
14. *Theaetetus,* 174.
15. *Laws,* 649.
16. *Euthydemus,* 291.
17. *Republic,* 534.
18. *Parmenides,* 162.
19. *Republic,* 534.
20. *Republic,* 500.
21. *Ibid.,* 537.
22. *Topics,* 101a35.
23. *Ibid.,* 101b1.
24. *Ibid.,* 100b20.
25. *Meta.* IV. 310005b19.
26. E. v. Hartman, *Über die dialektische Methode* (Berlin: Carl Dunker's Verlag, 1868), pp. 9-10.
27. *Meta.* IV. 2 1004b25: ἔστι δε ἡ διαλεκτικὴ πειραστικὴ περὶ ὧν ἡ φιλοσοφία γνωριστική.
28. *Ibid.,* 1004b19.
29. Plotinus, *Enneads,* Bk. I, 3:1-5. On the dialectic of Plotinus cf. Marcel de Corte, *Aristôte et Plotin* (Paris: Desclee de Brouwer, 1935), pp. 177-227; 229-290.
30. *Ibid.*
31. II. 13. 38. Pl. 32, col. 1013.
32. *Of Christian Doctrine* II. 31.
33. *Ibid.,* II. 37.
34. *Confessions,* Book X, ch. 6. Cf. also *On Psalm* 26, Serm. 2, 12; ACW 29, 272-273.
35. *Ibid.*

36. *De Trinitate,* XII, 21.

37. Cf. *Contra Academicos,* 3, 14, 31. *The Fathers of the Church* (New York: Cima, 1948), vol. 5, 204-5.

38. *Ibid.,* 3, 13, 29; p. 202.

39. Cf. *Confessions,* Book xiii, xi, 12: "For I am and know and will. . . ."

40. *The Divine Names,* tr. C. E. Rolt, *Dionysius the Areopagite on the Divine Names and the Mystical Theology* (New York: Macmillan, 1940), chap. I. pp. 53, 60, and *passim.*

41. PL 122, 510D.

42. *Ibid.,* 462C.

43. *Ibid.,* 686.

44. *Ibid.,* 526A.

45. J. G. Sikes, *Peter Abelard* (Cambridge: University Press, 1932), p. 50 ff.

46. *Sic et Non.* PL. 178, col. 1349A.

47. *Ibid.,* 1349B.

48. *Dialectica,* edit. L. M. De Rijk (Assen, Netherlands: Van Gorcum, 1956), p. 470, 4.

49. *Ibid.,* 470, 6-8.

50. The unity of all reality is well represented in the Gospel Book of Abbess Uota of Niedermünster in Regensburg, Plate XV, *Early Manuscript Illumination.*

51. On analogy in St. Thomas, cf. Gerald B. Phelan, *St. Thomas and Analogy* (Milwaukee: Marquette Univ. Press, 1948); also Ralph M. McInerny, *The Logic of Analogy* (The Hague: Martinus Nijkoff, 1961).

52. Cf. Alexander Koyre, *From the Closed World to the Infinite Universe* (Baltimore: Johns Hopkins Press, 1957), p. 8.

53. Nicolas Cusanus, *Of Learned Ignorance,* tr. Fr. Germain Heron. (London: Routlege & Kegan Paul, 1954). Book I, ch. 3, p. 12.

54. *Ibid.,* p. 11.

55. *Ibid.,* Book I, ch. 4, p. 12.

56. Cf. Eduard Zellinger, *Cusanus-Konkordanz* (München: Max Hueber Verlag, 1960), pp. 90-91.

57. Cf. *On the Infinite Universe and Worlds,* tr. Dorothea Waley Singer, *Giordano Bruno: His Life and Thought* (New York: Henry Schuman, 1950), p. 253 ff.

58. *Op. cit.,* 369.

59. *Inferno,* Canto VIII, 100-02. Ciardi trans.

2

TRAVELLER ON THE ROYAL WAY: MARTIN LUTHER ON *SIMUL JUSTUS ET PECCATOR*

An entire catalogue of statements from Luther's writings could be constructed excoriating that barren dialectic of the schoolmen which he saw as only obscuring the Gospel. It was the Aristotle of the *Organon* as well as the Aristotle of the *Metaphysics* that Luther had in mind when he changed the dictum *"Sine Aristotele non fit theologum"* to *"Cum Aristotele non fit theologum."* From Berengar to Siger of Brabant the revived art of dialectic had come to dominate philosophy and speculative theology. The scholastic method centering upon argument and disputation was based on Aristotelian logic or dialectic; it moved through a strict pattern of question *(quaestio),* argument*(disputatio),* and conclusion *(sententia).*[1] Luther lectured on dialectic, *the* method of discovering and illuminating theological truth. He sensed that it led one only to opinions, never to certainty. He came to dread the proud spirit of all dialecticians.

Yet there is a dialectic in Luther, which presupposes two points of view, as did the famous Socratic dialogue, and these points of view for Luther, too, diverged not merely superficially but on essential matters. On no subject is this more valid than in the life of faith: here the truth *must* be arrived at by way of con-

frontation of one expressed truth with a contrasting truth; it is not one, simple thing that must be said about the life of the believer. The *simul* is significant in this connection because no single proposition, stating either the *justus* or the *peccator,* conveys God's final judgment. Existentialist truth, a truth that conveys a proper understanding of existence, is arrived at only by way of supplementing a partial or limited truth with an opposing statement: the assertion "God takes me to be righteous" can and must be supplemented by the opposing assertion "God takes me to be sinful."

Luther and St. Paul on Man

The great reformer's deepest thought concerning man is summarized in the succinct formula *simul justus et peccator:* it embraces his analysis of natural man and of the new man in Christ. For Luther the formula summarized the profound struggling which characterizes the life of faith. Yet the biblical sources should serve as a check and critique for all formulations, including this famous expression from Luther.

Our examination will be a study in the history of Christian thought and will attempt to interpret the phrase *e mente auctoris.* The systematic theologian will have to deal with the whole complex of arguments raised by Krister Stendahl when he concludes, "this formula cannot be substantiated as the center of Paul's conscious attitude toward his personal sins. Apparently Paul did not have the type of introspective conscience which such a formula seems to presuppose." [2] Although Luther was not equipped with the "rather robust conscience" of a St. Paul we must be grateful to Luther the barbarian, the man who for the sake of Christ and the Gospel was willing to go to extremes, in order to chart most penetratingly the depths and limits of life lived in obedience to the Word.[3] It was this *simul justus et peccator* that served to protect the Gospel from the natural *opinio legis* on the one hand and from antinomianism on the other.

We shall examine our topic from the perspective of an experiential dialectic of sinner and saint. This perspective is not imposed upon Luther, but rather emerges from his writings, particularly the early commentaries on Scripture, but also from

his later works.[4] We shall investigate the *simul justus et peccator* especially as it appears in the exposition of Romans, since it is here that Luther gives classic and basic expression to the Christian's existence as "unsaintly sinner." Nowhere in Christian literature do the antinomies present in the Christian life emerge more vigorously than in these lectures of 1515-1516. Within the context of this chapter we shall not be able to set Luther's formula against the background of Pelagianizing late Medieval doctrines of justification.[5] It may suffice to say here that Luther's formula effectively breaks the continuity involved in the emphasis that God has committed himself to reward man's best efforts, the Nominalist teaching regarding the *"facere quod in se est."*

Dialectic and Dialogue

Luther's thought is at once dialectical, involving two points of view, and dialogical, involving two arguers. His vigorous and persistent arguments with the devil are well known to his students. To the devil's threats he could say: "If you find sin in me, you will find no sin in Christ, who is mine. So let me alone." [6] Luther's entire theology is a "dialogical theology"—dialoguing with the heretics, with the papists, with Erasmus, with the Biblical writers, and with himself. The Christian life is for Luther precisely this life of discussion, or inner dialogue, in which both sinner and saint arrive at the unsteady harmony which is the life of faith. Thus Luther writes in his "Third Disputation against the Antinomians:"

> John 3 asserts: "No one born of God commits sin," and yet the same author says, "If we say that we have no sin, we deceive ourselves." How is this? How do these things agree? How do these harmonize (*concordant*)—to be holy and yet to pray for sin? It is truly an astonishing thing. It is a most remarkable thing! Let him who can, make these rhyme: two opposites *(duo contraria)* in a single subject and at the same moment of time. [7]

Luther sees here a conjunction, operating simultaneously and repeatedly, of two irreconcilable elements.[8] This is no timeless truth describing the whole human situation but an ever-renewed

struggle between faith and sin. The Christian lives always as *forgiven* sinner. Repentance for sin stands between these deadly oppositions and operates as another *simul:* "always a sinner, always penitent, always righteous" *(semper peccator, semper penitens, semper justus)*. For by repentance a man becomes righteous from his unrighteousness." [9] Here we see the force of the first of the 95 theses: the believer is to "do penance" throughout the entire course of his life, not merely in certain specific acts of penance. The key connection here is confession of sin and the longing to be justified—not a soul-searching preoccupation with guilt or the fatuous entertainment of some sinless state.[10]

Rather than complain about this intolerable contradiction Luther chooses to acknowledge that "God is marvelous in his saints, who are at the same time righteous and unrighteous." [11] At this point human wisdom cannot venture to reduce the one truth into the other; there is no transition of the one into the other. Luther was content to leave these irreducible tensions—righteous/unrighteous—in experience and thought unresolved; he was sure that the "wonderful working of God" was sufficient explanation for this. Just as psychiatrists assure us that a healthy personality depends on the ability to conduct a running conversation with oneself, so the life of faith depends on the inner conversation between the man always inclined to rely on himself and the man ready to trust in God. Moreover, as the psychiatrist tells us that danger is present when normal conversation within the self breaks down, so Luther warns against a spiritual breakdown which occurs when the conversation between the man who "fears God" and the man who is confident in an already-achieved righteousness breaks down. Because this conversation was conducted so vigorously and, one must add, so consistently, Luther is an example of remarkable spiritual health rather than of a sickly spirituality.

Herein lies the significance of the proclamation of God's Word as condemning and forgiving the sinner. Just as the believer must say both things regarding himself so the preacher must communicate both God's condemnation of sin and the forgiving grace of God's love.[12] For it should be kept in mind that it is not only the believer who says both things regarding himself and not only the preacher, who, as God's "prompter," says these things about

him, but it is *God* who dispenses mercy through his justice. Were it not for the case that one has, ultimately, to reckon with what God's Word says to and about oneself he could remain comfortably ensconced in a life of monologue. But life is sustained and nurtured through the word that is "proclaimed:" it is no indifferent thing if *both* truths regarding the self, truths in the sight of God, come to be expressed to the individual.

Features of the Dialectic

There are three features of Luther's dialectic which deserve to be emphasized: it was a) experiential, b) profound, and c) sustained. It was experiential in that it expressed what had passed through the alembic of Luther's own experience. Luther held that every believer must continually live from and by God's truth as addressed to him. Because Luther discoursed so vigorously with himself regarding the tensions between saintliness and sinfulness he was convinced that he had an insight into the Gospel which must be spoken to and for others. He was not afraid to emphasize the role of his own personal decision in learning at the school of the Holy Spirit. He could do this while recognizing fully the gift of God from outside himself.[13] One of the most telling critiques of Luther's spirituality rests on the contention that in Luther the element of personal commitment is too strongly emphasized.[14]

The dialectic was profound because these are the most significant affirmations that can be made about a man: they are made of man "*coram deo*", "in the sight of God" or "in the presence of God".[15] Any other significant statements made of man "coram deo" are either parallel to or complementary to these statements. Luther refused to break this dialectic because of his acute awareness of the continuing truth of each opposing statement. In other words, this is no Kierkegaardian dialectic of Either/Or. The "*et*" of the formula must always remain, in the sense of "both-and." Each affirmation is valid of the Christian until he is translated from the church militant into the church triumphant. While he remains in this life faith requires a truly *militant* stance. Nor can one pole of this tension be permitted to dominate the other, as, for example, the "super-ego" of Freud comes to dominate the seething animal drives

of the "id." Sin continues to exercise its power also in Christ's saints. Any effort to minimize the range or persistence of concupiscence in the redeemed represents a compromise of the gospel.

Alternatives to Justus et Peccator

One might choose to examine Luther's dialectic in its operation between the law and the gospel; indeed, the dialectic present in law and gospel is always operative in the life of faith. Both are dynamic activities of God and whatever unity is to be found in them must be traced back to their source in God, though such unity remains forever inaccessible to man. One could argue, simply and surely, that the law-gospel antithesis became characteristic of Luther's thought only later, that it received definitive expression in the 1531 *Lectures on Galatians* and is not determinative for the 1515-1516 *Lectures on Romans.* But more to the point is the fact that the *simul justus et peccator* formula is an existential assertion—involving and expressing Luther's personal existence—of dynamic *proclamations:* [16] the law "reveals sin" or "makes sinners;" the gospel "presents Christ" and "makes righteous." No conflict exists between the two formulations: when dealing with the law one is in the province of Christ's alien righteousness, a righteousness of sheer mercy, and thus of impeccable saintliness.

Or one might see Luther's dialectic as operating between the sinner and God; however, if the opposition were to be studied from within this perspective it would have to be seen, for Luther, in the relationship between the righteousness of man and the righteousness and truth of God; this is not the Kierkegaardian dialectic between finite man and infinite God. The same man is aware of being acted upon by God and of being unworthy even in his noblest achievements. But if we choose to observe the dialectic in the setting of the individual believer, keenly aware at once of his wholly unsaintly character and of a hidden righteousness, we are not forsaking either of the above perspectives. We are rather committed to study them in their own matrix, for theology, when it speaks of God, speaks simultaneously of man. It exists *pro hominibus,* or as Irenaeus states in his classic declaration,

"Gloria Dei vivens homo" ("It is God's honor and joy that man should live.")

Nor are we ignoring or subverting Luther's key understanding that man is justified before God by faith alone. The two teachings affirm the same thing. Faith clings to the "alien righteousness" of Christ when one is "reckoned righteous" by God. But it is well to note how Luther affirms the role of faith, too, in determining the sinner. He writes:

> Even though we recognize no sin in ourselves we must, nevertheless, believe that we are sinners. This is why the apostle writes: "I am aware of nothing against myself, but I am not for that reason justified" (I Cor. 4, 4). For as through faith the righteousness of God lives in us, so through the same faith sin, too, lives in us, i.e., by faith alone we must believe that we are sinners, because it is not obvious to us; on the contrary, more often we are not aware of it. Therefore we must stand before the judgment of God and believe his utterance when he tells us that we are sinners, for he cannot deceive us. [17]

Here, too, God works *e contrario,* by contrasts. In his hatred of sin God is an angry God; he employs his wrath to consume the world, but God's anger can become an expression of his love. Thus his foreign work becomes God's proper work of benevolence and love. He humbles those whom he raises up, as he humbled Christ before all the world on the cross; the suffering was itself the glory. To be sure, the mob is easily deceived by appearances and is misled by the outward prosperity of carnal men. Therefore, says Luther, one must *believe* that the church is holy, though one sees that it is sinful, so one confesses "I believe a holy church," not "I see a holy church." [18] Unfaith is always tempted to capitulate before repeated misfortunes. The victory is always and only the victory of faith.

Duo Homines

The dialectic of Luther is not external to the individual: it cuts into the depths of the believer's being to constitute two men, the old and the new: *"duo homines, vetus et novus."* [19] Yet Luther

could hardly be understood to hold a hydra-headed view of man; the person is finally a single center of will and responsibility. It should be noted, first, that Luther understands himself as simply following the Apostle Paul and St. Augustine; the latter he credits with insight on this point which is at once unique, profound, and correct. Secondly, he notes that to the extent that the old man is dead in us we are dead to the law, and subjection to the guilt and power of sin has been broken. Therefore if the old man in us is dead we are dead to the law as well, for it no longer makes us subject to sin but it has lost its power in us.[20] Through the work of Christ the claim of the law as demand was removed because it had been perfectly fulfilled. Although the old man is still established as "old" and unregenerate by the law, yet because and in so far as the Christian serves the new man he is free from the tyranny of the law.

In the experience of justification Luther was conscious of a heavenly reality brought to coexist with an earthly reality. Historical action by God prior to and distinct from the believer's faith is coupled with existential appropriation. Doubt concerning the possibility of such opposites existing simultaneously can be overcome only through faith's overwhelming assurance of one's own unworthiness and Christ's total worthiness. Faith experiences in the most compelling manner possible the realization that, as St. Ambrose said, "I am always in sin," *(Semper pecco)*,[21] yet forgiveness is equally real. The believer is a sinner in fact but at the same time righteous through the reckoning and certain promise of God that he will free man from sin until he is altogether whole, "and in this way he is altogether whole in hope, while in fact he is a sinner." [22] Reason is left unsatisfied in the face of these two truths which must be said of one and the same man. Agreement is not forthcoming. They are opposed as the cherubims facing one another at the mercy seat. Only here, but most certainly here, they are united.[23] God is no deceiver. Though human language, human wisdom, and even human courage cannot rest in the face of such verities yet the believer experiences an assurance which is altogether adequate to enable him to hold to both affirmations.

Man as Peccator

It is man who is perpetually deceiving himself, i.e., is a liar, because he vaunts his own righteousness and virtue. We must come to agree with God's view of us, which sees us for what we really are, as in the wrong before his exacting standards.[24] Whereas faith should enable us to live with insecurities the refusal to admit our sin means that we "presume a false innocence." [25] We thus settle down in a "pestilential security." [26] Luther does not deny the presence of, nor advise against the exercise of, good and holy works. He points out, however, that in conjunction with the performance of such "righteous works" we develop a false estimation of their value: we put such confidence in them and hold them in such high esteem that we think God, too, must regard them as adequate before his standards. They should stand, rather, as our "petitions for righteousness." Thus when Luther insists that we "must become sinners" *(oportere peccatores fieri)*, he is calling for a sober and prudent evaluation of our own pitiful performances. We prefer to understand ourselves as living righteous and quite acceptable lives; we must adopt God's understanding of ourselves which would make us inwardly acquiesce in the view that we are sinners who are living in the wrong. Again here, in pointing to God's righteousness, which he alone powerfully effects in us, Luther emphasizes the sovereign power of God at work in the believer.[27]

Peccata Magnificare

One must rather "establish, increase, and enlarge sins" *(peccata statuere, augere et magnificare)*.[28] For this is the entire purpose of Paul's letter to the Romans, to destroy all our own wisdom and righteousness, since these are so apparent to us, and to set forth another reality, that of sin, since we are so unaware of its existence.[29] St. Paul writes against those who are confident of their own merit and thus have little need for the grace of God. Such confidence takes many forms, since the devil is an "artist of a thousand devices!" [30] But whether he chooses presumptuousness or complacency, insensitivity or hypocrisy, his devices must be unmasked and made to stand for what they are. Wilhelm Pauck identifies

Luther's discovery of the gospel precisely with this "taking seriously" of God's grace and man's sin as the Reformer summarizes it in a marginal gloss:

> In this letter, the apostle does not speak against those who obviously are sinners through and through but against those who in their own eyes are righteous and thus are confident that they will be saved by their works. It is these people he tries to lead to the realization that they must take the grace of God more seriously *(inducere ad magnificandam gratiam Dei),* but one cannot take it seriously unless one first acknowledges and takes seriously *(magnificatur)* the sin that is forgiven by it. This is why some were scandalized by this when they heard about it. They thought that the apostle was preaching that one must do evil in order to magnify the glory of God. But, as a matter of fact, our iniquity and falsehood 'abound to his glory' when, humbling ourselves by confessing them, we glorify God for the sake of his abundant grace as he forgives us our sins. [31]

Role of the Law

The *simul justus et peccator formula* derives its vigor from the force of the law in human life. Luther held to the continuing validity of the law in order that the Gospel itself might not be deprived of its power. Against the Antinomians he wrote: "Therefore the teaching of the law is necessary in the Church and is certainly to be retained, for without it Christ cannot be retained.[32] In his "Disputation against Scholastic Theology" Luther approached the question from another perspective: the law causes sin "to abound." Man's will is exasperated before the requirements of the law.[33] Luther experienced the law as a demand made on him by the Holy God. For Luther's colleague Karlstadt the Spirit made it possible for man to fulfill the law; the power of the Spirit fulfilling the law elicited in the believer a passion for holiness. Faith and law are identical for the justified. No contradiction exists any longer between what the law requires and what the man who has fled to grace desires.[34] For Luther, however, it is always impossible for man to fulfill the law. Nomological existence involves dependence on man's native gifts, what is "in us." Since this comes from the self it easily pleases the self. Further, it pleases so well that the sinner prides himself and boasts in his gifts. He must

emphasize the good he does or the evil he avoids, thereby misleading himself into thinking that he satisfies God's law. Faith involves a surrender of this proud security, an undoing of the self-determination which is so dear to us, and a reliance on the undeserved mercy of God.

Man's propensity toward evil derives from the nature of evil itself: it is no quiescent quality but is a restless evil, *inquietum malum*. In the face of evil of such vitality man's freedom of will, the freedom to do what is acceptable to God, is a mere figment of the imagination.

Luther saw clearly that it is impossible for man to fulfill the law's demands; the theological use of the law is to convict men of sin. It always and uncompromisingly requires fulfillment, yet by virtue of its arousing of lust it produces the opposite of self-giving love which is required. It leads, then, to despair. On the basis of the antithesis involved in the statement that *lex est negatio Christi* [35] Luther loved in his commentaries on the Psalms to contrast Moses with Christ. The law is the word of Moses. Thus Luther interprets Moses as "a minister of prison, a teacher of drudgery, and originator of servitude," and, following St. Paul, "a minister of death, sin, and sadness." [36] The joy of the gospel is revealed by "that better Teacher," Christ.[37] When Christ in man's stead fulfilled the law he did not cancel the law but he rather instituted that new and dynamic righteousness "by which he makes us righteous, just as the wisdom of God is that wisdom by which he makes us wise." [38] One cannot understand the radical character of the Christian's righteousness unless he recognizes Luther's "causative interpretation" of Biblical expressions.[39] God's righteousness is no dead or static quality in God; it is always dynamic application or imparting to "barren" man of God's active goodness. Thus a very restless evil is opposed by an altogether adequate and dynamic righteousness.

Man as Justus

In Luther's understanding, unless the depths are present the heights of the Christian life will correspondingly fail to emerge. In order to do full justice both to the capacity for sin present in

the saint and to the remarkable presence of the work of Christ in the sinner he explores more fully and heightens the oppositions present. Existence under the gospel entails dependence on God's "naked mercy." It is "outside us" or "in Christ." Yet it is "in us coming from him." [40] It is "reckoned" to man by a merciful God, yet in such a way that it is not an extrinsic thing. The term "extrinsic" here does not mean that righteousness does not really belong to the Christian, but it points to the difference between what we are in ourselves *(intrinsece),* in our own eyes or in our own estimation, and what we are *extrinsece,* before God and in his reckoning.[41] Since the gospel is the power, wisdom, and the righteousness of God at work in weak and foolish and unrighteous men it must remain hidden, buried, and not apparent. This was the pattern of the prototype, Christ, in whom God's power, wisdom and goodness were completely hidden, revealing only weakness, foolishness, and severe suffering.[42] Here, again, Luther heightens the opposition. The good man must fear, if he fails to encounter persecution, hatred, and adversity, that his work does not please God. Their very tribulations are a great comfort to the saints.[43] These trials will magnify positive qualities: the spiritual man will become more spiritual, the good man will become better.[44]

Totus Justus, Totus Peccator

The question thus arises as to whether the *simul* is to be understood as finding man partly a sinner and partly righteous, or is man completely sinner and completely righteous? Is the formula to be understood in the sense of *totus justus, totus peccator,* or as *partim justus, partim peccator?* It should be clear from the foregoing that before God neither the righteousness of Christ granted the believer nor his sinfulness before the law lack anything in completeness. Luther states: "For this is true, that by the divine reckoning we are in fact and wholly righteous *(totaliter justi),* even though sin is still present . . . Thus also we are in fact and wholly sinners *(totaliter peccatores)*." [45] Luther saw the formula as a protection of the fullness of Christ's righteousness. In this sense the opposition takes place between complete and exclusive entities; it is an opposition between true opposites.[46]

This "total aspect" of the *simul* forms the basic view of Luther; he goes beyond what St. Augustine could say when his tutor declared that the believer is "partly" righteous and "partly" sinner.[47] Luther's emphasis differs from that of St. Augustine both because of Luther's insistence that concupiscence remains as selfishness and thus as sin itself rather than as the spur to sin, and because of Luther's emphasis on the completeness of Christ's righteousness in the redeemed.[48]

But there is an opposition of a *partim, partim* nature also present in Luther. In his "Theses against the Antinomians" he writes: "In so far as Christ is risen in us, to that extent we are without the law, sin, and death. In so far, however, as he is not yet raised, to that extent we are under the law, sin, and death."[49] Thus Christ carries on the sharpest conflict in the believer, a conflict waging back and forth until death, against the flesh. In his exposition of the seventh chapter of Romans, Luther spells out this conflict, as when he says: "Therefore I am at the same time a sinner and righteous, because I do evil and I hate the evil which I do." [50] The Christian faith introduces one to a life of conflict not found in the natural man; the natural man is simply "fleshly." Here are two masters, each asserting authority:

> See how one and the same man at the same time serves the law of God and the law of sin, is at the same time just and sins! For he does not say, "my mind serves the law of God," nor "my flesh serves the law of sin," but he says, "I, this whole man, the same person, I serve a double servitude." *(totus homo, persona eadem, servio utranque servitutem)*.[51]

Here Luther might appear to break the tension when he introduces, by way of analogy, the concept of the *communio idiomatum.* Qualities proper to the flesh are attributed to the spirit, and vice versa:

> But because one and the same man is made up of flesh and spirit he attributes to the whole man both the opposites that come from the opposite parts of him. Thus there is introduced a *communio idiomatum:* one and the same man is spiritual and "fleshly," righteous and a sinner, good and evil.[52]

In fact, however, there is no confusion of the natures or mixture of the qualities proper to each; there could be no confusion of such active antagonists. But it is in one and the same person that the lively contest goes on. The antitheses remain.

The Christian Life as Becoming

However, if the Christian life is such a struggle waged between the new man in Christ and the old man serving sin, must the struggle always be inconclusive, always fluctuating between soul-sickness and health? Luther loved to compare the Christian to a sick man being healed by Christ, the Good Samaritan. The sick man has complete confidence when the physician assures him of a certain recovery:

> Then is this sick man already well? No, he is rather at the same time both sick and well. He is sick in fact, but he is healthy by virtue of the sure promise of the physician, whom he believes. For he reckons him as already healthy because he is certain that he will cure him; he has begun to cure him and he does not reckon his sickness unto death. In the same way our Good Samaritan, Christ, brought his patient, the man who was half-dead, to an inn, and began to heal him, promising him most perfect health in eternal life.[53]

By virtue of the sure care of such a physician the healing has the certain character of a "becoming." There is movement here between two conditions:

> One cannot understand this dialectic *(utrunque)* better than through the parable in the gospel of the man left half-dead. For when the Samaritan poured wine and oil on his wounds he was not healed immediately, but he began to get well. So, too, our sick man is one and the same man who is weak and is yet being healed.[54]

Here, as Joest points out, we meet "no longer merely an oscillating leap from nothing to everything, but also a continuous progress from less to more." [55] Sin still remaining in the flesh is no longer imputed to the man being healed. Thus condemnation is removed.[56] In his exposition of the twelfth chapter of Romans,

Luther clearly points to the manner in which faith transforms the mind:

> Here the apostle speaks of progress, for he is speaking to those who have now begun to be Christians. Their life is not a static matter *(in quiescere)*, but is in motion *(in moveri)* from good to better, just as a sick man is in movement from sickness to health, as our Lord also shows in the half-dead man whom the Good Samaritan took care of.[57]

Thus there can be a progress according to which the old man is daily put down and buried and the new man daily comes forth and arises, always through the effect of making man righteous. The believer is led to a growing recognition of God's will for him. It is God's purpose that man's will should be actively enlisted in the struggle against evil; he is led to a clearer recognition of God's will. The fact that progress is involved here is clear from Luther's language: "from day to day, greater and greater" *(de die in diem, magis ac magis)*.[58] Here Luther could quote Aristotle approvingly: man is always in not being, in becoming, in being *(non esse, in fieri, in esse)*.[59] Such becoming originates in faith and is nurtured by a faith which carries on the struggle in the "grey zones" of everyday life.

Problems in the Simul Formula: Only in Hope?

But if the saint is righteous *"in spe,"* is this *only* in hope? Luther's critics have not been hesitant in questioning the reality of such a righteousness which always bears about the counterpart of unrighteousness, which, indeed, is always "hidden" beneath its opposite. Does Luther's answer, that "though the remission of sin is indeed real, sin is not taken away except in hope, i.e., that it is in the process of being taken away by the gift of grace which begins this removal, so that it is only not reckoned as sin," [60] do justice to the New Testament conception of saintliness, and, secondly, does it allow for the sentiment of filial trust, the *parrhesia* which characterized man's restoration to Paradise through baptism, to arise? [61] These are questions of the greatest significance for theology. We must recognize that Luther's later controversy with

the Enthusiasts prevented him from developing an adequate doctrine of the Holy Spirit, but did the *simul justus et peccator* prevent such a development from the outset? Is there no integral role for the gifts of the Holy Spirit in the face of such lively oppositions?

We cannot enter here into the problematics of these questions. It should be said for Luther that sin had an obtrusive reality, but forgiveness was on this account no less real. No one can impede God.[62] This hope is of such a nature that it is always being realized. It lacks external evidences to support it; one must trust when the opposite of what is hoped for looms before one's eyes.[63] But though faith is difficult, i.e., is always a struggle, there is no question regarding possession of Christ's righteousness:

> And if He has made my sin his own, then I have it no more and I am free. If, moreover, He has made his righteousness mine, then I am righteous with the same righteousness as he has. However, my sin cannot swallow him up but it is swallowed up in the infinite abyss of his righteousness, for he is God himself who is blessed forever.[64]

Just as there is nothing lacking in the completeness of the saint's holiness, so there is nothing lacking in its valid, present appropriation. The guilt of sin is removed *propter Christum,* as is also the punishment for sin. Luther emphasizes that concupiscence remains as sin; it is selfishness and as such is not motivated by love of God. Yet this, too, is not reckoned against the man who longs for mercy.

No one rejoiced more vigorously than Luther in the peace and joy of believing; the *laetitia* of forgiveness was never far from Luther's consciousness. Though unbelief would continue to challenge the security of belief yet faith had its certainty and paradisaical assurance, because Christ is no deceiver. Yet it must be said that Paul Althaus does not account sufficiently for the deep inner contradiction in the life of faith when he concludes, "We cannot, from the alleged pessimism of the reformers, appeal to the more complete assurance of triumph of the ancient church." [65] The renunciation of Satan and the *pompa diaboli* and the reception of the *sphragis* did impart a sense of present victory to the candidate for baptism in the early church. [66] Luther sees only the "opposites"

of righteousness and wisdom, i.e., sin and foolishness, as apparent to the believer. [67] The life of the saint has a most "unsaintly" character, the sense of triumph bears the stamp of defeat in life's battles:

> For our good is hidden, and that so deeply that it is hidden under its opposite. Thus our life is hidden under death, love of self under hatred of self, glory under shame, salvation under perdition, the kingdom under exile, heaven under hell, wisdom under foolishness, righteousness under sin, strength under infirmity. And, in general, every affirmation of good is made under its negation, that faith might have its source in God, *who is the negative essence and goodness and righteousness whom we cannot possess or attain to except by way of the negation of all our affirmations.*[68]

The Royal Way

Luther's view of the believer as *simul justus et peccator* stands as his summary of two categorical structures of reality. On the one hand, he could derive both assertions from his own experience: in his struggles for faith, in the *tentationes,* these truths appeared as apparent inconsistencies. Honesty regarding himself demanded acknowledgement of his wholly unsaintly character; but faith witnessed to another reality conjoined in the most intimate manner possible to the first. On the other hand, Luther could derive these assertions from another structure of reality, distinct from but not unrelated to the first: theological analysis of God's will for man presented him with conceptual incongruities. He must recognize that through the same divine justice that convicted him of sin the grace of God emerged. In his willingness to span these inconsistencies and incongruities—in life and in thought—lies the immense vitality of Luther's perception of Christian man.

This was the "royal way" Luther was destined to travel. [69] He also calls this the *"via pacis in spiritu."* We cannot but be impressed by the anxieties present in travel on such a way, but it is much to Luther's credit that he did not seek peace first and then righteousness, but he sought righteousness and in this found peace. The words of St. Paul drew from his own experience the suggestion of a lovely antithesis:

> The righteous man has peace with God but affliction in the world, because he lives in the spirit.
>
> The unrighteous man has peace with the world but affliction and tribulation with God, because he lives in the flesh.
>
> But just as the Spirit is eternal, so the peace of the righteous and the tribulation of the unrighteous will be eternal.
>
> And just as the flesh is temporal, so the tribulation of the righteous and the peace of the unrighteous will be temporal.[70]

In walking this way Luther learned to know and hate sin and to walk in the fear of God. It preserved him from false security and presumption on the one hand and from despair of self and God on the other. One may describe travel along this way in terms other than those which Luther used, but one may well question whether there is any other way.

Notes

1. Cf. David Knowles, *The Evolution of Medieval Thought* (Baltimore: Helicon Press, 1962). 87 ff.
2. Krister Stendahl, "The Apostle Paul and the introspective Conscience of the West," *Harvard Theological Review* LVI (1963), p. 202. Cf. Karl Holl, "Die Rechtfertigungslehre im Lichte der Geschichte des Protestantismus," *Gesammelte Aufsätze zur Kirchengeschichte,* III, 534.
3. Paul Althaus says of Luther's interpretation of Romans 7: "It is exegetically impossible, it contradicts the thought of Paul, but it expresses the self-judgment of the Christian in a way that we must substantially accept." *Paulus und Luther über den Menschen,* 3 erweiterte Auflage (Gütersloh: Carl Bertelsmann Verlag, 1958), p. 94. For the difference between Luther and St. Paul see also Wilfried Joest, *Gesetz und Freiheit: Das Problem des Tertius usus legis bei Luther und die neutestamentliche Parainese,* 2 Auflage (Göttingen: Vandenhoeck & Ruprecht, 1956); and *idem,* "Paulus und das Luthersche *Simul Iustus et Peccator,*" *Kerygma und Dogma* I (1956) 269-320; Ragnar Bring, "Die paulinische Begründung der lutherischen Theologie," *Luthertum* 17 (1955), 18-43; Gerhard Ebeling, *Word and Faith* (Philadelphia: Fortress Press, 1963), 247 ff; Karl Barth, *Christ and Adam* (New York: Collier Books, 1962), *passim.*
4. To cite the key occurrences of the formula in the *Römerbriefvorlesung,* see: 56, 70, 9: *Ideo simul sum peccator et justus;* 272, 17-18: *simul peccator et justus; peccator re vera, sed justus ex reputatione et promissione;* 57, 165, 12: *simul justus et simul peccator, peccator scilicit re vera, sed justus ex fide promissionis et spe impletionis.*
5. Cf. Heiko A. Oberman, *The Harvest of Medieval Theology* (Cambridge, Mass., 1963), 425 ff Also *idem,* " 'Iustitia Christi' and 'Iustitia Dei,' Luther and the Scholastic Docrtines of Justification," *Harvard Theological Review* LIX (1966), 1-26.

6. Commentary on Psalm 45, *Luther's Works* (St. Louis: Concordia Publishing House, 1955), vol. 12, p. 260.
7. *WA* 39 I, 507, 18—508, 2.
8. Gerhard Ebeling, *Luther, Einführung in sein Denken* (Tübingen: V.C.B. Mohr [Paul Siebeck]), p. 260. Tr. by R. A. Wilson as *Luther, An Introduction to his Thought* (Philadelphia: Fortress Press, 1970). Ebeling warns that the Reformer's distinction between law and gospel should not be read as a difference between two kinds of doctrinal content. *Op. cit.,* p. 257.
9. *WA* 56, 442, 17-18.
10. *WA* 56, 266, 13 ff.
11. *WA* 57, 164, 7. Cf. also 39 I, 515, 2.
12. *WA* 39 I, 355, 5.
13. Wilhlem Pauck, "Luther's Faith," *The Heritage of the Reformation,* revised and enlarged edition. (Glencoe, Ill.: The Free Press, 1961), p. 25 ff. *Cf. WA* 55, 22, 16, 2 ff.
14. Joseph Lortz, *Die Reformation in Deutschland* (Freiburg: Herder, 1939-40), I, 120 and *passim.*
15. Gordon Rupp, *The Righteousness of God* (London: Hodder & Stoughton, 1963), 154 ff. For two positive evaluations of the *simul* formula on the part of Catholic scholars see Karl Rahner, "Gerecht und Sünder zugleich," *Schriften zur Theologie* 6 (Einsiedeln, 1965) 262-76, and Reinhard Kösters, "Luthers These 'Gerecht und Sünder zugleich,'" *Catholica* 18 (1964) 48-77, 193-217; 19 (1965) 138-62, 171-85.
16. Gerhard Ebeling, *Luther, Einführung in sein Denken,* 128 ff.
17. *WA* 56, 231, 6-12.
18. Commentary on Psalm 45, *Luther's Works,* vol. 12, p. 234.
19. *WA* 56, 65, 17.
20. *WA* 56, 65, 22-23.
21. *WA* 56, 274, 2.
22. *WA* 56, 272, 19, *"Ac per hoc sanus perfecte est in spe, in re autem peccator."*
23. *Works,* vol. 27, 231.
24. *WA* 56, 229, 7—230, 8.
25. *WA* 39 I, 348, 19.
26. *WA* 39 I, 349, 9.
27. *WA* 56, 232, 34—233, 33.
28. *WA* 56, 3, 6-11.
29. *WA* 56, 157, 2-6.
30. *WA* 56, 266, 19.
31. WA 56, 33, 13-22. The translation is Pauck's, *Lectures on Romans,* vol. XV, Library of Christian Classics (Philadelphia: The Westminster Press, 1961), pp. xxxiv-xxxv.
32. *WA* 39 I, 357, 29-30.
33. Prop. 74, Martin Luther, *Early Theological Works,* vol. XVI, Library of Christian Classics (Philadelphia: The Westminster Press, 1962), p. 271.
34. Cf. Andreas Bodenstein von Karlstadt, *De spiritu et litera,* ed. Ernst Kähler (Halle: Max Niemeyer Verlag, 1952), v1; 75, 30-33. Kähler comments on this point: "The last statement applies, indeed, not because and in so far as the justified man believes in Jesus Christ but because he has entered into

inner possession of the grace which is bound up with the law." *Ibid.*, xl. For a penetrating study of the operation of this contrast between letter and Spirit as it appeared in the earliest form of Luther's thought, revealed in the first exposition of the Psalms, 1513-15, see Gerhard Ebeling, *Luther, Einführung in sein Denken,* 100 ff.

35. *WA* 40 II, 18, 4.
36. *Works,* vol. 12, 205.
37. *Works,* vol. 13, 78.
38. *WA* 56, 262, 22-23.
39. Cf. Gerhard Ebeling, "Die Anfänge von Luthers Hermeneutik," *Zeitschrift für Theologie und Kirche,* 48 (1951), 228 ff.
40. *WA* 56, 173, 25.
41. *WA* 56, 268, 27 ff.
42. *WA* 56, 171, 14-18.
43. *WA* 56, 196, 20.
44. *WA* 56, 301, 5-7.
45. *WA* 39 I, 563, 13-14; 564, 3-4.
46. Cf. Wilfried Joest, *Gesetz und Freiheit,* p. 58: "It is not the case of a no-longer-wholly-sinful person being joined to a not-yet-wholly-righteous person in a psychologically comprehensible mixture; it is rather the case of real and complete righteousness being opposed to real and complete sin."
47. Pauck, *Lectures on Romans,* xliv.
48. *Ibid.*, xliv-xlv.
49. *WA* 39 I, 356, 17-20.
50. *WA* 56, 70, 9-10.
51. *WA* 56, 347, 2-6.
52. *WA* 56, 343, 16-19.
53. *WA* 56, 272, 7-13.
54. *WA* 56, 351, 17-20.
55. Joest, *Gesetz und Freiheit,* 68.
56. *Works,* vol. 27, 227.
57. *WA* 56, 441, 14-17.
58. *WA* 56, 443, 5-6.
59. *WA* 56, 442, 15.
60. *WA* 56, 274, 8-11.
61. Cf. Jean Daniélou, S.J., *The Bible and the Liturgy* (Notre Dame, Ind.: University of Notre Dame Press, 1956), 35 ff.
62. *WA* 56, 295, 26-27.
63. *WA* 56, 295, 19 ff.
64. *WA* 56, 204, 19-23.
65. *Paulus und Luther,* p. 94.
66. Cf. Daniélou, *op. cit.,* 20 ff.
67. *WA* 56, 393, 3-12.
68. *WA* 56, 392, 28-393, 3.
69. *WA* 56, 283, 7-12.
70. *WA* 56, 298, 8-15.

3

MUSICIAN IN THE CONCERT OF GOD'S JOY: JACOB BOEHME ON GROUND AND UNGROUND

Jacob Boehme (1575-1624) conveys his novel and daring insights through a profusion of symbols and metaphors. The reader is repulsed when he sets out to integrate theories from alchemy, figures from Scripture, and the play of poetic fantasy when exploring the implications of words. But the impossibility of framing a congruent "system" from his impassioned intuitions of the contradictory aspects of reality should not blind one to insights which are themselves congruous, trenchant, and highly influential. Schelling was to turn to Boehme for his positing of "first potency" as dialectical nonbeing in God. In his *Lectures on the Philosophy of History,* Hegel was to acknowledge his own deep indebtedness to the *teutonicus philosophus.* Schopenhauer's appeal to the creative force of the will owes much to Boehme. English literature alone would furnish an impressive catalogue of Boehme students: William Law, Coleridge, and William Blake. In our own day his influence is traceable as well in the panpsychism of Charles Hartshorne, in Tillich's "Ground of Being," in the meontic freedom of Berdyaev, and in the primordial *Nichts* of Heidegger.

It is a strange development which finds a simple, self-instructed tradesman, an heir of Luther's reform, providing a philosophical

explication for those very mysteries which Luther had reserved to faith. Much as Luther stands in the history of Christian thought as a preeminent example of pistic theology, accentuating faith's unquestioning trust against the claims of reason, Boehme the shoemaker stands as an example of gnostic theology, asserting comprehension of the data of faith on the part of reason. [1] Where Luther was content simply to accept the presence in God of both wrath and love, Boehme gave a metaphysical basis and interpretation of these "realities of faith," read now as contradictions rather than as contrasts. And whereas Luther resolved his agonizing in the face of God by directing himself to "der Mann Christus," Boehme was preoccupied with the gnostic quest, "Whence the birth of God?"

A Philosopher among the Simple

Boehme was sensitive to the stumbling block which his "simplicity as an author" would constitute for his readers.[2] Luther had reminded himself that such questions are reserved for the holy angels or the divine intelligence alone. Boehme states that originally it had never entered his mind that one so simple should be writing for anyone but himself. [3] He wrote to provide himself a "memorial" of God's marvelous workings. Only contrary to his will were copies made and circulated. [4] He labored under the incongruity that he was "a philosopher among the simple." [5] He was treating divine and sublime topics, and he appeared to lack any qualifications; but in his economy of salvation had not God often used unlettered workmen to correct the falsifying *literati:*

> What was Abel? A shepherd. What were Enoch and Noah? Simple people. What were Abraham, Isaac and Jacob? They were tenders of cattle. What was Moses, that dear man of God? A tender of cattle. What was David, when the mouth of the Lord called him? A shepherd. What were the prophets great and small? Ordinary and humble people, some of them only rustics and herdsmen, the very footstools of the world. They were accounted as mere fools. . . . And how did our King Jesus Christ come into this world? Poor and in great grief and misery, and had no where to lay his head.[6]

Boehme senses parallels to himself in these mean people. The

learned doctors, on the other hand, showed the character of the wise when they called for the crucifixion of Christ. Boehme's own storming of heaven becomes less incongruous in the light of such predecessors—*surgunt indocti et rapiunt caelum.*

Boehme was conscious of standing in the tradition of Luther's re-forming. Luther had, indeed, purged lust for money, idolatry, bribery, and deceit from the churches in Germany. As "a poor, despised friar" he had withstood learned scribes and powerful ecclesiastics.[7] But the dawning of the new day, even the morning redness before the full dawn, should never be identified with Luther's *Turmerlebniss;* it was reserved for that "triumphing in the spirit" which gave rise to Boehme's *Aurora.* He asks:

> What is still concealed? The true teaching of Christ? No, but the "philosophia" and the deep ground of God; the heavenly pleasure; the revelation of the creation of the angels; the revelation of the horrible fall of the devil; from whence evil proceeds; the creation of this world; the deep ground and mystery of man and of all creatures in this world; the Last Judgment and change of this world; the mystery of the Resurrection of the dead; and of eternal life.
>
> This shall arise in the depth, in utter simplicity. Why not in the height, in art? In order that no man might dare to boast that he himself had done it, and that thereby the devil's pride might be disclosed and brought to nothing.[8]

He invites his reader to read his book with care, that he might share in the dawning of the new day and be ready for the eternal, heavenly wedding. God's love would have men walk in the pure, luminous, and deep knowledge of God. [9]

Dialectic within God

Boehme's dialectic penetrates all that is: God, the world, and man. Already in his earliest work, the *Aurora,* which was begun on New Year's Day, 1612, but recording a mystic sunrise which had been gestating for 12 years, his attention spans the nature of God and the totality of beings. He could not comprehend "the deep births of God in their essence." [10] He was thrown into a deep agony of perplexity. [11] Why do contradictions pervade everything? Why do the godless enjoy prosperity as great as that of the

godly? Because of such *Grundprobleme* he was "altogether melancholy and deeply troubled, so that no Scripture could comfort me." [12] He pored over "the great deep of this world, also the sun and stars, the clouds, as well as rain and snow" and in everything he found good and evil, love and wrath, possessing a priority of being and metaphysical ultimacy. [13] Should there be any question regarding the gnostic character of Boehme's speculation—*speculari* in its original, positive significance of philosophical seeing—one must examine the break-through of his spirit, at the conclusion of an immense assault "upon God and all the gates of hell," into "the most intimate birth of the Godhead." [14] It was "comparable to nothing so much as that in which life is born in the midst of death; it is comparable to the resurrection of the dead." [15] It was something most extraordinary that was imparted to him at that moment, for Boehme says:

> In this light my spirit suddenly saw through everything, and in all creatures, even in the herbs and grass it recognized God, who he is, and how he is, and what his will is. And suddenly in that light my will was seized by a great impulse to describe the essence of God. But since I could not at once comprehend the deep births of God in their essence, and grasp them in my reason, at least twelve years transpired before the proper understanding was given me.[16]

Boehme finds "two qualities, one good and one bad, which are in one another as one thing in this world, in all powers, in the stars and the elements, and no creature in the flesh, in the natural life, can subsist without having both qualities in it." [17] He proceeds to stipulate the meaning of this key term "*Qualität*" as "the mobility, surging, or driving of a thing." [18] It is the thing's characteristic feature, which operates as a "*Quell,*" a spring or source, in everything. Only the pressure of a counter-quality or counter-will can—to the accompaniment of *Qual,* birth pains and tribulation—allow for the emergence of something's *Qualität.* Thus must contradictory qualities interact upon one another to produce one thing, *qualificiret unter einander wie ein Ding.* [19]

Boehme builds the opposition between God's wrath and his love to extreme limits, or, rather, to the point where no limitation or proportion remain. Each opposes the other as omnipotent:

> For just as his wrath is almighty for destruction, so is his love also almighty for preservation; if this "Contrarium" did not exist, then there would be no life and no good, and no evil either. Now, however, the essence of all essences is revealed, so that what is good or evil is made visible. Thus the essence of all essences is a continual acting, desiring, and fulfilling: fire desires light, in order that it may have humility and the nature for its burning or life, and light desires fire, otherwise there would be no light, and it would have neither strength or life. . . . Therefore I say to you: God's love is as great as his wrath, his fire is as great as his light . . . everything is equally eternal, without beginning.[20]

Boehme was quite capable of recognizing the logical contradiction inherent in "two almighties" in the Deity. But he wished to point to the dynamic activity in the divine life itself.

Dialectic within the Self

This gigantic conflict within the Godhead has its counterpart in the self, where Boehme finds one's own will *(eigener Wille)*, which is the self-assertive will directed toward multiplicity, and the resigned will *(gelassener Wille)*, directed inward toward unity. The creative character of the opposition between these two wills becomes evident by the fact that each is necessary for the existence of the other. Only in the face of opposition, by overcoming opposition, can the will—which is, indeed, free in its choice—realize its own individuality. Only the man who has asserted himself in seeking his own egotistical satisfactions, then has been reintegrated into the purposes of God by being reborn through faith, can possess the harmonious will to effect God's inclusive plan under alien conditions.[21] The opposition between selfish desire and resignation to the divine will is nowhere more complete than in Boehme: the only solution to the Babel of the soul's unrest is that one become "as a nothing," that he abandon his personal will so that God's will may unify his self.[22]

The Dialectic of Divine Birth

In his probing of the hidden mystery of being Boehme saw both being and the possibility of not being. The affirmation of

the presence of being always has its counterpart in awareness of its absence. Description of the divine being required, for Boehme, delineation of the theogonic process by which three persons derive from the one and the natural world stems from the Trinity. It is not the Father who begets the Son from all eternity, but the one "begetteth himself in himself, from eternity to eternity." [23] The origin of the Supreme Spirit is characterized by Boehme as an "eternal stillness," *(eine ewige Stille ohne Wesen).* [24] Were it not replete with desire it would be a Nothing, nothing would be stirring or drawing itself forth. But an inner necessity, a Will, impels it, so that this first Will "beholds itself," i.e., elicits a second and contrary Will.[25] This process does not take place in the temporal order, in some succession of moments, but, as in Hegel, it occurs as a logical function in the divine life. Our mind requires pictorial representation of "stages" in this movement, but the total simultaneity and organic unity of the theogonic process should not be ignored. [26] Moreover, the terms Boehme employs are not to be understood conceptually; they point symbolically to something beyond every particular thing and beyond all that can be named. Any predicate affirmed of such terms is inadequate by virtue of their universal relationships.

Even—and supremely—in God the experience of a contrary is required if "something" is to be consciously known, for it is axiomatic that "Nothing without contradiction can become manifest to itself; for if it has nothing to resist it, it goes continually of itself outwards, and returns not again into itself." [27] The divine depth must be reflected in the mirror of the *logos,* so that the divine can see itself, become an object standing over against itself as subject, so that the divine might know itself—as *homo faber* comes to know who he is only by expending his efforts on something outside him. So God can enjoy the richness and variety of his own internal life only through the three centers of the trinity—austere and angry as Father, loving and compassionate as Son, fashioning, shaping, completing as Holy Spirit. [28] And the formation of the physical world is not a *creatio ex nihilo,* an act by which God posits something outside himself, but rather creation from himself, a manifestation from the No-thing of God. As such the world is something other than God, the result of a free divine

fiat, though certain of Boehme's formulations place him uncomfortably close to the Neoplatonic "generation." Separate and particular modes of being are themselves not divine but are "figures," modes of revelation of the hidden life of God. The emphasis on continuity, on continuous development, is greater than orthodox Christian teaching regarding discontinuity between God and creatures would allow.

Ungrund and Grund

Boehme's dialectical conception of *Ungrund* and *Grund* emerges here. The *Ungrund* is the endless, undifferentiated, unoriginated "source" of the divine life itself. It is "grounded" in nothing whatsoever, so that in relation to particular, formed, dependent things it can best be termed a "No-thing." Yet the *"ewige Nichts"* is heavy with desire. It craves the attainment of a *Grund:*

> The unground is an eternal nothing, but makes an eternal beginning as a craving. For the nothing is a craving after something. But as there is nothing that can give anything, accordingly the craving itself is the giving of it, which yet also is a nothing, or merely a desirous seeking.[29]

The "No-thing" desires to become concrete rather than potentially concrete, to receive form rather than remain formless, to become something, an *"Etwas,"* instead of its bare "No-thing." Without the will for "Some-thing" the "No-thing" could not exist, nor could "Some-thing" exist without the "No-thing." The craving, Boehme says, is "*All,* and yet as a Nothing." [30] Its gaunt emptiness yet embraces the richness of endless possibilities; so from the perspective of formed or limited being it is replete with limitless freedom; it *is,* for Boehme, precisely this boundless freedom. Though enjoying such complete freedom, being still undefined and indeterminate and void of passion, it nevertheless craves the attainment of self-consciousness. It covets a more significant awareness of its own identity. The mystery of this juxtaposition of "freedom" and "need," of "passionless repose" and "restless craving," of *Ungrund* and *Grund,* of "will" and "counter-will" is never "explained," other than to point to the actualization of the self, through opposition by an "other," into a greater fulness—which nevertheless adds nothing to what was already present.

The dialectic does not, however, cease when the formless has acquired form and self-consciousness, so that it may find and feel, love and know itself.[31] It seeks to slough off all limitations of form through a new birth.[32] So it must pass through "death" to newness of life: it must overcome the limitations of form through the redemption of form.

A Will to Self-actuation in God

Boehme's "No-thing," which is the power of being, must be distinguished from the nondialectical nothing, the pure non-being, which the Greek language denominated οὐκ ὄν. The οὐκ ὄν is the idea of not-existing. It is "nothing" in the most complete sense of the term in the sense of the *creatio ex nihilo,* since the Greek negative οὐ is the particle which summarily negates in contrast to the qualified denial of the weaker negative μή. This οὐκ ὀν is a non-being existing outside of God and bears no relationship to being. It is the unqualified negation of being, complete absence of being. What Boehme speaks of is the μὴ ὄν, the "No-thing" which stands in a dialectical relation to being. It is the divine nothingness which is not privation of being but potentiality of being. This dark, primal, unconditioned abyss "sees" and "discovers itself" as conditioned being:

> Seeking then the first will is an ungroundedness, to be regarded as an eternal nothing, we recognize it to be like a mirror, wherein one sees his own image; like a life, and yet it is no life, but a figure of life and of the image belonging to life. Thus we recognize the eternal Unground out of Nature to be like a mirror. For it is like an eye which sees, and yet conducts nothing in the seeing wherewith it sees; for seeing is without essence . . . We are able then to recognize that the eternal Unground out of Nature is a will, like an eye wherein Nature is hidden; like a hidden fire that burns not, which exists and also exists not. It is not a spirit, but a form of spirit, like the reflection in the mirror. For all the form of a spirit is seen in the reflection or in the mirror, and yet there is nothing which the eye or mirror sees; but its seeing is in itself, for there is nothing before it that were deeper there.[33]

God manifests himself to himself in this procession from *Ungrund* to *Grund.* The procession becomes God's means of attaining consciousness of himself—through the *Grund* that reveals God's pure potentiality to himself. The presence of the unfathomable, timeless will within this *mysterium magnum* reveals Boehme's voluntarism. God strives to actualize the vision of his splendor as reflected in the mirror. His will reacts upon the products of his imagination and craves to actualize them. For the divine psychology must conform in a supereminent way to its image in man. [34] Nature, which had been excluded from God in the Hebrew encounter with the surrounding nature-gods, is brought into the Godhead once again. Potentiality is present within the Godhead, rather than the pure actuality of St. Thomas' conception of God. For St. Thomas there can be no potentiality in God because God supremely and eternally is everything he may become, but for Boehme the eternal will in God continually gives rise to all that is: will is the source of self-actuation in both God and in man. St. Augustine had, indeed, raised the question of novelty in God. How, he asks, is one to understand the strange genesis of creatures? In *The City of God* he raised Boehme's problem, "this extremely difficult question of how, in view of his eternity, God could produce new things without any novelty of will." [35] He recognized the problem, but fell back upon faith rather than drive toward knowledge.

Moreover, as has been indicated, Boehme's God is not absolutely simple, like the God of St. Thomas, but is guilty of composition: the totality of Being includes evil as well as good, darkness as well as light. For the classical theism of St. Augustine or St. Thomas such negativity within God is simply anathema: God is the sovereign exception to all negativities and potentialities. For Boehme the perfection of God simply demands that he is not altogether simple. Self-manifestation, self-consciousness, self-realization are all possible simply because there is dialectic within the divine:

> The reader should know that in Yes and No all things consist, whether it be divine, or demonic, earthly, or whatever may be named. The One, as the Yes, is pure power and life, and is the truth of God, or God himself. He would be unknowable in himself, and there would be no joy, or exaltation, or feeling, in Him without the No. The No is the

> counterstroke of the Yes, or the Truth, in order that the Truth might be manifest and a something, in which there might be a *contrarium,* in which the eternal love might be active, feeling, willing, and something to be loved. And yet one cannot say that the Yes is separated from the No and that they are two things distinct from one another, for they are but One Thing, but themselves divide into two Beginnings (Principia) and form two *Centra,* since each works and wills in itself. Without these two, which stand in perpetual conflict, all things would be a Nothing, and would stand still without movement.[36]

This defense of dialectic from Boehme's last, unfinished work, which breaks off after the answer to the fifteenth in a series of 177 questions into the sources of revelation, deserved extended quotation and careful examination. Evidently in the marvelous quarter-hour of illumination a comprehensive symbol reconciling the contradictions was provided Boehme. The mighty contraries remain. There is efflux of vital energy, and contravention, and retrogression into the enriched center once again, but so intimate is their intervention, so dependent are they on one another that a unifying process of development emerges. There is eternal birth in the Godhead.[37] And this theme of the geniture of God would always weave its thread through Boehme's speculation, just as one finds a parallel interest, his predilection for symbols of life and growth, fruit trees, flowers, beasts—all illuminating the theme of life-process. It is the theogonic process itself that holds Boehme's powerful antitheses within God, nature, and man together. In place of static opposition Boehme sees development and growth emerging from constructive opposition: light emerges from darkness, and love triumphs in its conflict with anger in God. One element interacts upon another to produce healing and wholeness. It became a metaphysical principle that without contradiction and strife ". . . there would be no nature, only an eternal stillness and no will; for the contrary will gives rise to movement."[38]

Final Reconciliation

However, for Boehme, quite contrary to Luther, God as he really is, is never wrathful nor does he punish. A true imagination,

one formed by light, recognizes that God is all Love and Light and Goodness, though in his dealing with the sinful world the powerful *contrarium,* the wrath of God, is manifest. For a true imagination recognizes that the Father is never apart from the Son. A false imagination thinks of the Father as existing alone and as such he can be known only as wrathful, angry, jealous. Sin, too, is then the imagination of the thought of fallible creatures. It has reality to the man who imagines it, but in itself it is no positive thing.

The Silesian seer saw himself as one of the strings in the concert of God's joy.[39] God's spirit played upon him ceaselessly, producing dissonance and melody. Was it Dionysius rising from the depths of being to sing a song of ecstasy, or was it Christ descending once again in history from the heights to sing a litany through a servant-shoemaker? As source of that dialectical method which became the instrument of Schelling, Novalis, and Hegel, he inspired a chorus of Dionysian voices. He is echoed in the antiphonies of Angelus Silesius' *Cherubinic Wanderer:*

> Ich bin so gross als Gott, Er ist als ich so klein;
> Er kan nicht über mich, ich unter ihm nicht sein.[40]

Yet in his own commitment Boehme saw himself as a faithful instrument of Christ. In fact, both Dionysius and Christ are to be found in his rapturous melodies, and it is difficult to say at any particular point whether Christ or Dionysius sings through him. His weakness was the weakness of all gnostic theologies, i.e., the tentatives of faith are subverted. His strength was the strength of a supremely gnostic system. In this system the cobbler-mystic has few equals.

Notes

1. On the interrelationship of the two, cf. Heinrich Bornkamm, *Luther und Böhme,* Bonn: A. Marcus und E. Weber, 1925.
2. *Aurora, oder Morgenröthe im Aufgang,* 9, 1. *Sämtliche Schriften I* (Stuttgart: Fr. Frommanns Verlag, 1955), p. 104.
3. Ep. 1, 2-3. *Sämtliche Schriften* IX; p. 1-2. Cf. also Ep. XXI, 1-2; p. 84.
4. Ep. 8, 61. *Unterricht von den letzten Zeiten an Paul Kaym. Sämtliche Schriften* V, p. 415.
5. *Aurora,* 18, 80. *Sämtliche Schriften* I, p. 256.

6. *Ibid.*, 9, 3-4; p. 104.
7. *Ibid.*, 9, 7; p. 105.
8. *Ibid.*, 9, 8-9; p. 105.
9. *Ibid.*
10. *Ibid.*, 19, 14; p. 266.
11. *Ibid.*, 19, 5; p. 265.
12. *Ibid.*, 19, 9; p. 266.
13. *Ibid.*, 19, 5 and 6; p. 265. Hans Grunsky identifies "the great deep of this world" with the infinity of space which Boehme confronted in the Copernican world-view sometime prior to 1600. Cf. his *Jacob Boehme* (Stuttgart: Fr. Frommanns Verlag, 1956). p. 19 ff.
14. *Ibid.*, 19, 11; p. 266.
15. *Ibid.*, 19, 12; p. 266.
16. *Ibid.*, 19, 13-14; p. 266-67.
17. *The Aurora,* tr. John Sparrow, ed. C. J. B. and D. S. H. (London: James Clarke & Co., 1960), pp. 39-40.
18. *Aurora, oder Morgenröthe im Anfang,* 1, 3; *Sämtliche Schriften* I, p. 24.
19. *Ibid.*, 1, 15; p. 27.
20. *Gegen Tilke II,* 2, 142-43; *Sämtliche Schriften* IX, p. 132.
21. Cf. Howard Brinton, *The Mystic Will* (New York: Macmillan, 1930), p. 212 ff.
22. Cf. *De Signatura Rerum,* 15, 24-35. *Sämtliche Schriften* VI, p. 221-23.
23. *Mysterium Magnum,* 1, 2. Tr. John Sparrow, ed. C. J. B. (London: John M. Watkins, 1924) I, p. 1.
24. *Vierzig Fragen,* 1, 6. *Sämtliche Schriften* III, p. 9.
25. *Ibid.* 1, 13; p. 10.
26. Cf. *Von der Gnadenwahl,* 3, 10. *Sämtliche Schriften* VI, p. 27.
27. *Of the Divine Intuition,* 1, 8. *Six Theosophic Points* (Ann Arbor: Univ. of Michigan Press, 1958), p. 167.
28. Cf. Hans Lassen Martenson, *Jacob Boehme: His Life and Teaching,* tr. T. Rhys Evans (London: Hodder and Stoughton, 1885), pp. 93-4.
29. *Concerning the Earthly and Heavenly Mystery,* 1. *Six Theosophic Points,* p. 141.
30. *Mysterium Magnum,* 29, 1; p. 254.
31. *De Signatura Rerum,* 2, 6, 8. *Sämtliche Schriften* VI, pp. 9-10.
32. Cf. John J. Stoudt, *Sunrise to Eternity* (Philadelphia: Univ. of Pennsylvania Press, 1957), p. 231.
33. *Six Theosophic Points,* 1, 7-9; pp. 6-7.
34. Cf. Martenson, *op. cit.,* pp. 64-5.
35. Book xii, ch. 21.
36. *Betrachtung Göttlicher Offenbarung,* 3, 2-3. *Sämtliche Schriften* IX, pp. 6-7.
37. Cf. Grunsky, *op. cit.,* p. 25 ff.
38. *De Signatura Rerum,* 2, 1-2. *Sämtliche Schriften* VI, pp. 8-9.
39. *The Confessions of Jacob Boehme.* Compiled and edited by W. Scott Palmer (New York: Harper & Brothers, 1954), p. 164.
40. *Cherubinischer Wandersmann* (1657), Strophe 10, in Neudrucke deutscher Literatur werke. Herausg. V. Georg Ellinger (Halle: Max Niemeyer, 1895), p. 15.

4

PRODIGY BETWEEN FINITE AND INFINITE: PASCAL'S DIALECTIC OF GRANDEUR AND MISERY

Blaise Pascal (1623-62) is always the lively dialectician. Both the content of his thought and the form of its expression testify to this. He engages in dialectical argument with Epicurus, with the Stoics, with Montaigne, with Descartes. For him dialogue is rooted in the operations of nature, which alternate like the tide of the sea, ". . . *itus et reditus.* It goes and returns, then advances further, then twice as much backwards, then more forward than ever, etc." [1]

Pascal is distinctive in his ability to identify himself, both intellectually and emotionally, with extreme alternatives. He had explored the ranges, the applications, and the implications of Epicureanism and Pyrrhonism more thoroughly and more deeply than anyone else. These contradictions make his synthesis more pointed and direct than those of any other. He is catholic in his sympathy—in the original meaning of the word, "to be affected by the same feelings." He shared the diverse feelings of an *homme du monde,* of a research scientist, of a devoted follower of Christ. Though so remarkably universal in his sympathies, Pascal is wholly specific in his loyalty. Indifference, neutrality, these are the real offenders. The encounter with the holy and living God

in 1654 was itself a fusion of incandescent contrasts, the union of the experience of falling away from God, being forsaken by him, and the experience of joyful participation in the life of God, even ecstatic union with him. The awareness of total distance is present here, but there is an overwhelming sense of harmony through submission to "the God of Jesus Christ." He holds together not a single contradiction, not even a whole cluster, but a host of conflicting experiences—in mathematics, physics, engineering, philosophy, and theology. And how can this Pascal, who protests so passionately his adherence to the one, Roman, and Catholic Church, protest in the name of an evangelical faith barely tolerated there?

Dialectic in Place of Analogy

The *Apology* falls into two distinct parts, the first presenting man's misery without God, the second his happiness with God; or he suggests a parallel procedure, a first part proving that nature is corrupt, and a second establishing a Redeemer. Corruption can be established on the basis of nature, but redemption is to be demonstrated on the basis of Scripture.[2] He despairs of arriving at a rational grasp of the divine reality, as this formed the self-evident end of theological science in the tradition since Plato. For Pascal man no longer participates, as Plato contended, in the divine ideas; he is, therefore, unable to relate himself to the divine by imitating the divine *logos* imbedded in the world. Man is still the student of divine reality, but unless this reality reveals itself to him he remains confused and uncertain. The simple, unified cosmos of the Medieval world had been shattered by early modern philosophy and science. In its place appeared Bruno's infinity of unending universes, both large and small. Infinitesimal calculus had freed mathematics from its system of simple numbers. Before these abysses of infinitely large and infinitely small the *analogia entis* had lost its convincing power. John Donne was to deplore the loss of this world:

> 'Tis all in pieces, all coherence gone;
> All just supply, and all Relation.[3]

Descartes could still seriously speak of a "middle point," a "mean," in his understanding of man; man might still be seen as a "mean" situated between God and nothingness. But here a classic harmony of the contrasts no longer really exists. To be sure, Pascal, too, speaks of a mean when he describes man in nature, "A nothing compared with the infinite; a whole with regard to nothing, a mean between nothing and everything." [4] The mean here is something different from what it is for Descartes, for to Pascal "any appearance at all of the middle" has disappeared.[5] Man has lost his secure place in the universe. He has himself become a "prodigy" in the presence of prodigies.[6] Man is suspended between the infinite vastness of the starry universe and the infinite minuteness of sub-atomic universes; he is incommensurate with either—as our astronauts today experience their incongruity between the sophisticated systems of microcircuits around them and the vast ranges of space. They participate most intimately, one might argue, in both, yet their actual participation only serves to obscure the extremely limited participation possible to them. They are commensurable neither to Pascal's "nothingness" nor to the "infinite" that would engulf them. Their presence on our satellite moon must, in spite of their courage, evoke Pascal's naked horror, "The eternal silence of these infinite spaces frightens me." [7]

The accessibility of man to the truth is far less direct than he usually supposes. He is faced with inconceivables which must be tested. Pascal says:

> It is a natural weakness of man to believe that he possesses truth directly. For that reason he is always ready to deny anything which is incomprehensible to him. Yet, in fact, by nature he knows delusions only, and he ought to regard as genuine only the opposite of those things that seem to him to be false. That is why, whenever a proposition is inconceivable, we should suspend judgment and not deny it because of that; we should, however, examine the opposite. Then if we find this manifestly false, we boldly affirm the first proposition, however incomprehensible it may be . . . . for if these two opposites are both inconceivable, it is nevertheless necessarily certain that one of them is true.[8]

Pascal faced such inconceivables in grappling with the theory of the vacuum: both the proposition that this contained a "finer species of matter" and that it was really a void were unacceptable. A similar problem faced him in the concept of infinity, where he found himself confronted with agonizing contradictions of measure. His own perception of the contrariness of things led him to observe, "That makes me believe that there are springs in our head, which are so disposed that he who touches one, touches also the contrary." [9]

Pascal's Existential Dialectic

In addition to this cosmic dialectic in Pascal there is another, the locus of which is within man. The capacity of man's mind simply mirrors the disproportion of the vast extremes: our senses are not attuned to the extremes of experience; we can know no single segment of the universe because such knowledge would really require knowing the whole. However, a part cannot know all other parts: it can neither know the "imperceptible chain" binding disparate parts together nor the mysterious totality of all parts.[10] When one compares with this St. Thomas Aquinas' dictum regarding learning, that "The proper end of knowledge is the essence of material things," then it must be said that Pascal does not deny such an end as such. Yet because of the dislocations, the lack of harmony between man's intellectual equipment and the many-facetted world outside him, man *may* on occasion happen upon the truth. But he is much more likely to be deceived by such a fortuitous discovery—and thus to become insensitive to his many errors.

For there is a qualitative difference between the sphere of *les corps* and that of *les esprit.* Man may choose to live on the lower level or he may span the oppositions and rise to a higher level. One's powers of perception may be limited to phenomena and qualities of the material world, "But there are some who can admire only carnal greatness, as if there were no intellectual greatness. . . ." [11] These are the *grands de chair,* those who are essentially carnal-minded. It is senseless to compare them with those who live on the intellectual level. There is a splendor in

this lower level, as there is in each level; but intellectual greatness has a splendor far surpassing everything in the carnal sphere. Still there is another stage variously denominated *la charité, de sainteté,* or *le surnaturel,* to which "the infinitely higher *grandeurs de la sagesse*" corresponds. For a vaster difference separates the order of charity from spirit than divides the latter from the carnal, "All bodies together, and all minds together, and all their productions, are not equal to the least movement of charity. This is of an order infinitely more exalted." [12] A radical distinction in *genre* separates each of these orders from the other. But God himself must intervene through his revelation to grant access, by divine grace, to the supernatural stage. Romano Guardini in commenting on this emphasizes the similarity to Kierkegaard's "leaps" because of the distinct existential spheres:

> He must thus take the risk. Between the two levels lies an abyss, an obscurity. Man must, in the earnestness of the decision, gather himself together, raise himself out of himself, and throw himself across. Then he gains a footing and is able to exist on a higher level; his eyes are opened to a new and superior reality; a new power of evaluation awakens, and he is able to appreciate and to love on a higher level. Thus the existence of a truly living man is divided according to existential levels and the risks which lie before each level: according to "stages" which in each case bear their own values within themselves, pose their special problems, and in which corresponding possibilities of the given, concrete man are realized.[13]

Misery and Dignity

Pascal's dialectic examines the contradictory facets of man in order to bring them together into a whole.[14] The comprehensive concept that unites these facets is the *coeur,* the "heart." In the universes of this "heart"—roughly the mind's capacity for immediately perceiving, intuiting, and cherishing—stretch the vast distances, e.g., between dignity and misery. And in Pascal this dialectic in unity of the *extrémités* remains. The misery remains: the emptiness of man's purposes, the speciousness of his reasoning, and his little life-course—these are always present to him. Everything, apparently, conspires to mislead man: the senses overpower

the weak control of reason, and reason makes itself ridiculous in its claims to comprehend. Greater insight into the human heart simply reveals greater baseness and greatness. Pascal revels in describing the gambols of imagination, "that deceitful part in man." [15] The wisest, most just, most powerful, most healthy are all despoiled by the ploys of imagination. Yet one's playful imagination is but one among a host of self-deceptive propensities. Pascal is just as contemptuous of the inroads of self-love: we shelter ourselves from the truth that may be known by others or ourselves. We want to escape our miserable, imperfect, contemptible selves.[16] We love ourselves so much that we cannot bear to admit our faults; we devise intricate ways to shield our imperfections from ourselves and others. Our wretchedness appears just as clearly in our desire for ever-new diversions.[17] Were we really happy in our state of being we would not require such constant distractions from thinking about it.[18] These are not merely incidental distractions; they vitiate all our energies and contentment. No one is allowed to live happily or consider himself happy by this constant itch. And, in case these diversions should not be convincing enough, Pascal describes the ridiculous effects of vanity; the vain man is really a most miserable creature.

But man's dignity, too, remains. His dignity, his greatness, lies in thinking. Man at least *knows* that he is dying, that he is a miserable wretch while living.[19] And this intuition of his greatness simply expands the vast distances between his greatness and his vileness. For man is greatest when he *knows* himself to be most wretched. The important thing in man, then, is this conjunction of opposites, opposites which must be developed over their wide spectra and to their extreme expression, yet by avoiding their attendant vices.[20]

Reconciliation in Christology

Error always appears when one of the contraries—the recognition of excellence as well as of baseness—is suppressed: "All the principles of sceptics, stoics, atheists, etc., are true. But their conclusions are false, because the opposite principles are also true." [21] There is no simple unity or harmonization of the two, but there is a "middle point," the knowledge of Jesus Chirst. This is the

great prerogative of Christianity: it does not simply hold the two great truths regarding man in incompatible juxtaposition. It reconciles the negatives, not by reducing them to the same plane, as natural wisdom would have it, but by recognizing and by maintaining two levels, nature and grace, man brutalized and divinized. Man's weakness belongs to nature—a "fallen" nature, to be sure—and his grandeur belongs to grace. Thus the dialectic for Pascal the theologian is between two categories, nature and grace, and the *signum* for the union of the two in Christian man is the God-man:

> This is the astounding and novel union which God alone was able to teach, and which He alone is able to achieve. This union is but an image and an effect of the ineffable union of the two natures in the single person of a Man-God.[22]

Pascal's solution to the contradictions, these entire contrary universes stretching away from one another in the human heart, is thus Christological. It rests, for Pascal, in the *Mystère de Jésus.* It is not an obvious solution: it has the *incognito* to shroud him from those who fail to seek, and the *splendour* of majesty to reveal himself to those who diligently search. The universes within natural man are thus "answered" on this higher level by their counterparts in true religion, Christianity: "The knowledge of God without that of our wretchedness produces pride. The knowledge of our wretchedness without the knowledge of God produces despair. The knowledge of Jesus Christ forms the middle point; for there we find both God and our wretchedness." [23] A necessary truth of "true religion" is that it must delineate the basis of "these astonishing contradictions." [24] This is the great prerogative of Christianity, in contrast to natural religions and philosophy, that it sees man in his greatness and his wretchedness, and it knows the reason for both.[25] Again the Christological key, "In Jesus Christ all contradictions are reconciled." [26] As Luther found his *punctum mathematicum* in faith, devoid of all extraneous considerations, so Pascal finds his "imperceptible point" in the person of Jesus Christ. Jesus alone reveals man to himself, both in his infinite capacities for evil and in his character as *ad Deum creatus.*[27] At the heart of Christian faith are to be found these "two truths together:" there is a God, yet man is not worthy of

him. If one holds either of these truths alone he has either the God of the proud philosophers or he has the misery of the atheists. Each truth held separately distorts and destroys. But the Christian religion is itself the synthesis which reconciles these opposing truths about man.[28]

Pistic or Gnostic Dialectic?

The truth about man is thus no single, simple truth: it is multi-faceted and dialectical. Pascal develops his thought, for the most part, independently of Biblical data, on grounds which would convict natural, reasonable man of his misery. The brilliance of his intellectual *tour de force* can, however, detract from the convincing power which he himself, as a pistic thinker would accord the Biblical dialectic of Christological synthesis. His demonstration of the truthfulness and superiority of Christianity appears, at times, to be a gnostic emptying of the categories of faith. Still he declares that he seeks merely to "lead man to the desire of finding the truth." [29] The true religion which man seeks presents a truth about man which transcends his own understanding. If it were to exclude reason it would be surrendering to a credulous belief which would have to allow every crude superstition. If it were to confine itself to reason alone it would sink into a narrow deism or a truncating naturalism. By transcending reason religion preserves the fullness of reality—a fullness to which the Christian religion is better attuned than is the limited range of reason. One must agree with Jacques Chevalier when he concludes:

> Thus the Pascalian dialectic in no way denies reason, to raise faith upon its ruin. On the contrary, it is an endeavor to show that the Christian religion is eminently in conformity with reason, and that the latter must submit to it. . . . For the *logical* reason, then, Pascal substitutes the *reason of effects;* or rather, he subordinates logical reason to the reason of effects. . ." [30]

In the end, Pascal does not fit the category of either pistic or gnostic religion. His conception of faith, the "religion of the heart," transcending reason without contradicting it, includes aspects of both pistic and gnostic religiousness. The dialectic of natural man is a prolegomena to the dialectic of nature and grace; the one is a dialectic of "ignorant searching," the other one

of "confident finding." [31] Pascal asserts a remarkable congruence between what reason tells us about our wretchedness and greatness and the analysis a "true religion" makes of these phenomena.

Extending the Possibles

Throughout the life of the Christian these dialectics of error and truth, *misère* and *grandeur,* death and life, sin and holiness, are at work. Christian faith serves to expand and deepen the contradictions—far beyond anything experienced by natural man: "it humbles infinitely more than reason alone can do, but without despair; and it exalts infinitely more than natural pride, but without inflating." [32] So the effect of Pascal's dialectical view of man is that it extends the limits of possibilities far beyond anything a unilateral view could propose. He extended the range of man's sensibilities because he saw more that must be accounted for than contemporary schemes would allow. It is on this basis that he writes, "Things have diverse qualities, and the soul diverse inclinations; for nothing is simple, of that which presents itself to the soul, and the soul never presents itself simply to any object. Thence it comes that one weeps and laughs about one and the same thing." [33]

Faith is certainly confronted by clarity and by incomprehensibility. The clarity, however, never allows for the kind of comprehension that can transform faith into knowledge. Nature's witness to a Creator is equivocal; everything remains a matter of uncertainty, because the signs can be read either as pointing to a Divinity or to no need for a God. The wager itself points up the ambiguities of man's knowledge; it is a means to escape the dilemmas of reason, because "Reason can decide nothing here. There is an infinite chaos which separates us. A game is being played at the extremity of this infinite distance where heads or tails will turn up." [34]

Pascal is the tortured genius, the prodigy torn with passionate conflicts until he lapsed into the final long silence. Here is the form of the cross, the shaping of carnal man into the *conformitas Christi,* conformity to the passion and death of Jesus whom Pascal loved. The shame *is* the glory, the *misère* is the *grandeur* of a heart uniquely Christian.

Notes

1. *Pensees,* 355. Tr. W. F. Trotter (New York: Modern Library, 1941). Cf. J. H. Broome, *Pascal* (New York: Barnes & Noble, 1965), pp. 139 and 198. Broome characterizes Pascal's work as that of "an essentially synthesizing mind." Cf. p. 57 and *passim.*
2. *Pensees,* 60.
3. *An Anatomy of the World.* "The First Anniversary," 213-4.
4. *Pensees,* 72.
5. *Ibid.*
6. *Ibid.,* 434.
7. *Ibid.,* 206.
8. *The Mind of the Geometrician,* tr. Emilé Cailliet and John C. Blankenagel in *Great Shorter Works of Pascal* (Philadelphia: Westminster, 1948), p. 197.
9. *Pensees,* 70.
10. *Pensees,* 72.
11. *Pensees,* 793.
12. *Ibid.*
13. *Pascal for Our Time,* tr. Brian Thompson (New York: Herder and Herder, 1966; original edition, 1962), p. 21.
14. *Pensees,* 82.
15. *Ibid.*
16. *Ibid.,* 100.
17. *Ibid.,* 139.
18. *Ibid.,* 165.
19. *Ibid.,* 347.
20. *Ibid.,* 353.
21. *Ibid.,* 394.
22. *"Conversation with Monsieur de Saci," Great Shorter Works,* p. 131.
23. *Pensees,* 526.
24. *Ibid.,* 430.
25. *Ibid.,* 433.
26. *Ibid.,* 684.
27. *Ibid.,* 548.
28. *Ibid.,* 443.
29. *Ibid.,* 424.
30. *Pascal,* tr. Lilian A. Clare (New York: Longmans, Green and Company, 1930), p. 180.
31. *Pensees,* 432.
32. *Pensees,* 435.
33. *Ibid.,* 112.
34. *Ibid.,* 233.

5

THINKER OF THE THOUGHTS OF GOD: HEGEL AND THE DIALECTIC OF MOVEMENT

Hegel had high praise for Kant, the thinker who restored dialectic, yet it was Hegel himself who was to bring dialectic into its full inheritance. The term dialectic appears both in a pejorative and in a positive sense in Kant. He links dialectic unmistakably with sophistry when he surveys the dubious history of dialectic as a branch of logic. The ancients, Kant says, generally applied the term dialectic to sophistry, since, ". . . with them it was nothing else than a logic of illusion—a sophistical art for giving ignorance, nay, even intentional sophistries, the coloring of truth, in which the thoroughness of procedure which logic requires was imitated, and their topic employed to cloak the empty pretensions." [1] Dialectic in this sense is the unfailing fabricator of error. His own transcendental dialectic, then, sharpens the oppositions of prodigal reason into insoluble antinomies.

But Kant himself chooses to use the term "in the sense of a critique of dialectical illusion." [2] It is a critical exposé of the mind's excesses in dealing with non-physical matters. His own transcendental logic is "a critique of understanding and reason in regard to their hyperphysical use. This critique will expose the groundless nature of the pretensions of these two faculties . . ." [3]

His critical philosophy is an unmasking of the unwarranted extensions of man's judgment. Kant reveals the contradictions, the antinomies, into which reason permits itself to be misled. All of these contradictions can be "proved" by reason: that the world has a beginning in time and is limited in space, and its antithesis or self-contradiction; the second, that every composite substance consists of simple parts, and its antithesis; the third, which asserts the necessity of a causality of freedom, and its antithesis; and the fourth, which claims the existence of an absolutely necessary being, and its antithesis. [4] Reason moves beyond actual and possible experience when it "proves" such conclusions. Such an abuse of reason can establish *either* of two mutually incompatible conclusions. Kant saw his own insistence on the limits of speculative or theoretical reason as opening the way for belief in God as a postulate of practical reason.

Hegel acclaims the Kantian antinomies, but radicalizes them. The contradictions do not arise simply from a plague affecting man's understanding: they are not located simply in our thought and language, but are to be found in the "things in the world." [5] Dialectical movement pervades all of reality: the motions of the heavenly bodies, the dynamics of man's life in society, political life, where extreme anarchy and extreme despotism give rise to one another, and in the extremes within one's personal life, where pleasure and pain, laughter and melancholy, swiftly give way to one another.[6]

Movement in the Concepts of Pure Reason

Moreover, Hegel refused to accept the Kantian limitations of theoretical reason. The real and the rational he sees as sharing a common structure: they are pervaded by a common rationality, a common inner logic. On the basis of this coincidence of the real and the rational, thought can and does penetrate the essence of material things. Hegel is not breaking with the whole tradition of Western logic when he sees contradictions at the heart of reality. He is not contesting the Aristotelian principle of contradiction, which states that "A" cannot be "non-A." He is rather pointing to a many-sidedness of reality to which traditional logic does not

do justice. When an alternative in thought or action is developed to its full extent and implications, Hegel says, it is seen to be transformed into something quite different, possibly into a radically different perspective. Many of the concepts employed in logic he shows to be altogether inadequate, even to be caught up in radical contradictions. There are contradictions inherent in our cherished notions which would, if recognized and accounted for adequately, force us to adopt an alternative or more inclusive position than such a one-sided perspective. We usually suppress rather than admit such contradictions. Hegel's dialectic of movement sees concepts turn into their opposites, something *other* than they are, thus something to complete them:

> Wherever there is movement, wherever there is life, wherever anything is carried into effect in the actual world, there Dialectic is at work. . . . Everything that surrounds us may be viewed as an instance of Dialectic. We are aware that everything finite, instead of being inflexible and ultimate, is rather changeable and transient; and this is exactly what we mean by that Dialectic of the finite, by which the finite, as implicitly other than what it is, is forced to surrender its own immediate or natural being, and to turn suddenly into its opposite. . . . Dialectic is the universal and irresistible power, before which nothing can stay, however secure and stable it may deem itself.[7]

When Hegel applies this theory of dialectic to microcosmic and macrocosmic detail he frequently becomes vague and unsatisfactory, but the failures should not be permitted to detract from the movement, the various "figures" of dialectic. It must be noted that for Hegel philosophy begins not with this "life and soul of scientific progress" which is dialectic.[8] It begins with the very distinct, definite, and stable fixation of ideas and principles resulting from an exercise of thought termed the Understanding.[9] This is the first characteristic "moment" of philosophical thinking. All of the various sciences, arts, professions, and the everyday conduct of life are built on the processes by which Understanding distinguishes one idea from another, one assertion from another, one judgment from another. For thought as Understanding grasps objects in their distinct individuality, not in the concrete action of sensation or

feeling, but by analyzing and separating attributes of its subject. No knowledge—in the form of theory or practice—would be possible for Hegel without the fixation and precision which are the great merit of "mere understanding." [10] These limited abstractions of the Understanding are the essential, vitally-necessary components to be integrated into the second "moment" of the philosophical enterprise, Dialectic.[11]

Through Dialectic the finite determinations of the Understanding "work their own dissolution, and pass over into the opposite categories." [12] The one-sided abstractions of the Understanding press onward to be complemented in the Dialectical stage by a host of alternatives or by complementary possibilities, even by possibilities that are polar opposites:

> But by Dialectic is meant an indwelling tendency outwards and beyond, by which the one-sidedness and limitation of the formulae of understanding is seen in its true light, and shown to be the negation of these formulae.[13]

There is an inner solvent at the core of reality rather than stable unity. The concentration of the Understanding on limited particulars does not detect this, but there is a dynamic flux in all of life and thought, turning things even against themselves. This negative stage is completed for Hegel in what he calls Speculations, the positive stage in which the disharmonies of Dialectic are united in a higher unity by Reason, i.e., Speculative Thinking. Speculation absorbs the contradictions of dialectical thinking as well as the fixed abstractions of the Understanding. Hegel states:

> A one-sided proposition therefore can never give utterance to a speculative truth. If we say, for example that the absolute is the unity of subjective and objective, we are undoubtedly in the right, but so far one-sided as we enunciate the unity only and lay the accent upon it, forgetting that in reality the subjective and objective are not merely identical but distinct.[14]

Speculation unifies and conserves all the disparate threads of the preceding "moments" in a profound, avowedly mystical harmony. Just as the great mystics could overcome the contradictory affirma-

tions of cataphatic theology in the mystic harmony of an inclusive vision, so Speculative Thinking integrates experience and thinking in the depths of Reason. The contradictions of Dialectic are "annulled" only to be "preserved" in the mystic depths of a synthetic view.

Dialectic in The Science of Logic

We may at this point pass from the lesser logic to Hegel's larger and more comprehensive *Science of Logic*. Here he has an accolade for the German language because on occasion it unites not only various but opposite meanings in a single word. Such words demonstrate the working of Speculative Thought in the language, a phenomenon which only baffles the Understanding. As an outstanding example which functions at the center of his own method Hegel cites the word *aufheben* (to sublimate). The term is animated by the "speculative spirit" of the German language:

> *Aufheben* has in the [German] language a double meaning in that it signifies conserving, *preserving,* and at the same time also making cease, *making an end.* Even conserving includes the negative aspect that something is taken out of its immediacy, and thus out of an existence that is open to external influences, to be preserved.—Thus what is *aufgehoben* is at the same time conserved and has merely lost its immediacy but is not for that reason annihilated.[15]

Hegel, like Boehme, sees this "annulling" and "preserving" at the center of the divine life itself; a dialectical negativity is restlessly working in the self-realization of the Absolute Spirit. In the movement of reality from "yes" to "no" and on to "yes" again Reason reconciles the contradictions of Dialectic into higher unities. Reality is a dynamic process of becoming. Traditional logic does not account for time and change precisely because it does not understand contradiction in things; it falsely shifts contradiction to subjective reflection alone.[16] Hegel has in mind something quite different from the understanding of formal logic as reflected in the tradition from Aristotle to Kant, for he defines contradiction as "the root of all movement and life, and it is only in so far as it contains a Contradiction that anything moves and has impulse and

activity." [17] Findley clarifies Hegel's intention on this point when he states, "Hegel's main innovation is to connect the thought of such conflicting real or thought-tendencies with thoughts and modes of speech which are themselves expressions of such conflicts, and to suggest we should think and speak of the former by means of the latter." [18]

In *The Science of Logic* Hegel undertakes the examination of some of the one-sided yet key terms to point out their limitations. Dialectic embraces Being and Becoming, since Becoming is the unity of Being and Nothing. As Walter Kaufmann says when speaking of the concepts and categories of the *Logic,* "they are all one-sided abstractions from a concreteness of which they are merely partial aspects." [19] Hegel begins with what he considers primary, with a brief characterization of a fundamental category which has no specific character—with pure Being. Thus his starting point is the simple recognition that something is, without taking into account that what has being is determined in one way or another, differentiated in some manner within itself, or set apart in particular *things.* It is therefore what Hegel calls "immediate," i.e., it is not "mediated" by any relationship to determinate beings, such as quality, quantity, etc. But this is impoverished Being. It is "empty" of determination, so a nothingness of intelligibility. He says of this recognition of pure Being, "there is in it no object for thought, or again it is just this empty thought. In fact, Being, indeterminate immediacy, is Nothing, neither more nor less.[20] Since Being and Nothing coincide Hegel can delineate Nothing in terms indistinguishable from those used for Being. "Nothing" is contentless, undifferentiated, altogether lacking in determination. Being has "passed over" into the sheer absence of anything. Like the Nothing of Heraclitus and Boehme, this is the dialectical Nothing, standing in relation to Being. Hegel distinguishes it carefully from the non-dialectical Nothing which he sees as opposed to Becoming, a view which, he says, informs the abstract Pantheism of the Eleatics and Spinoza.[21]

Hegel proceeds to bridge the distinction still prevailing between Being and Nothing by the category of Becoming (*Werden*). Both Being and Nothing disappear immediately into their opposite. Thus Hegel can say, "Their truth is therefore this movement, this im-

mediate disappearance of the one into the other, in a word, Becoming; a movement wherein both are distinct, but in virtue of a distinction which has equally immediately dissolved itself." [22]

Nothing in the vast reaches of natural phenomena or human experience, whether this be sensuous experience or social process, the enterprises of man's theoretical or practical reason, is excluded from the dialectical movement which forms the Absolute. For it is only "the whole" that constitutes the truth.[23] And only at the grand *finale* of the magnificent human-divine-natural process of emergence will self-conscious Spirit have actualized itself: then Spirit will have become conscious of itself. All contradictions will have been mediated. This "whole" is composed of the totality of determinations or moments *(Momente)* of spirit which have appeared in nature and in history.

The Concrete Embodiment of the Idea

The master dialectician emerges from the realm of abstract ideas, from what he himself calls the "realm of shadows" in analyzing concepts in the two Logics, when he undertakes the description of self-consciousness in *The Phenomonology of Mind.* Here he enters another distinct branch of the philosophical sciences. Logic had dealt with the formal articulation of concepts predicable of reality as a whole. The abstract ideas studied in logic are now shown to be embodied in particular, concrete phenomena of Spirit and Nature. He is now at his best and the dialectic displays its lustre in the superabundant realm of persons; here *Mind* or *Spirit* appears on the dialectical stage. The self is here not simply conscious of objects in the external world, where sense-certainty affords only the most abstract, the poorest kind of truth.[24] The "moments" of the stage of consciousness have been annulled and are preserved as moments in self-consciousness.[25] Here the self is reflected in other living things and is thus given the opportunity to *see* itself. Only another self can "negate" myself, i.e., enable me to understand myself: "Self-consciousness attains its satisfaction only in another self-consciousness." [26] But this recognition of the other self, and of the self in the other, is incomplete so long as it does not recognize in this inescapable social nature of selfhood a superior self-consciousness,

"Mind" or "Spirit," which is, "the unity of the different self-related and self-existent self-consciousnesses in the perfect freedom and independence of their opposition as component elements of that substance. . . ." [27]

But the meeting of the self with another self involves, Hegel declares, a life-and-death struggle. Each self-consciousness proudly attempts to assert itself in the face of the other; it attempts to destroy the other even at the cost of being destroyed itself. Freedom is attained only via this ultimate risk, this willingness to stake one's own individual existence upon the destruction, or negation, of the rival's existence. Only through such a "trial by death" does authentic personhood emerge.[28] "Freedom" or "personhood" in this sense means the kind of "self-consciousness" which entails both a more complete *awareness* of one's self and a more adequate *assurance* of self.[29] Hegel expresses this also in terms of "cancelling the self" and being "sublated" and "preserved" in the other.[30]

But the outcome of the conflict cannot be equipoise between the two selves: the one accepts the dependent status of a slave rather than choose extinction. The slave exists for the other, though on the level of a thing—employed with the care of things. The master controls the slave and products of his work for his own enjoyment. Yet in this very lordship Hegel detects something quite different from the exercise of an independent consciousness: the master finds himself relying on the labor of the slave; the slave who confers value and form and permanence on things through the shaping activity of his toil and service attains a greater independence than the "contentless" independence of the presumed master. He "overcomes" the elements of his environment through his mediating labor in a way the master's empty enjoyment could never do. So he cancels his dependence and transforms his situation vis-à-vis the master precisely through his work.

Externalized Spirit in Stoicism, Skepticism, and the Unhappy Consciousness

Hegel next spells out the nature of this freedom on the part of self-consciousness by sketching its historical expressions in Stoic-

ism, Skepticism, and the Unhappy Consciousness. The free self-consciousness manifested in Stoicism rises, through the simple operations of thought, above the relations of master and bondsman.[31] The Stoic mentality appears on the scene of world history only when a curious conjunction of fear and bondage emerges alongside the highest cultural achievements.[32] But the self-sufficiency of the Stoic mentality remains abstract and without content. Skepticism gives flesh to the empty notion of Stoicism; it pushes the positive affirmations of Stoicism into its own consistently negative conclusions: Skepticism annihilates the very being of the world which the Stoic tried to address with his positive affirmations of virtue. But Skepticism possesses contradictions which St. Augustine had delighted in pointing out, "It announces the nullity of seeing, hearing, and so on, yet *itself* sees and hears. It proclaims the nothingness of essential ethical principles, and makes those very truths the sinews of its own conduct. Its deeds and its words belie each other continually . . ." [33]

The contradictions of Skepticism give birth to the Unhappy Consciousness. Here the self is conscious of the inner contradiction that rends it, whereas in Skepticism the division, though really present, remains unrecognized. Something of the longing and restlessness of St. Augustine's *cor inquietum* is reflected here by Hegel; the self is destined to live indecisively and incompletely between two worlds: it knows itself as belonging to the "unchangeable," to "ultimate essence," but it is bound to the "manifold and changeable as the unessential." [34] The illustrations Hegel vaguely and episodically adduces for this Unhappy Consciousness are particularly strained. For example, the three persons of the Holy Trinity each reflect aspects of this double consciousness: The Father, as the "first unchangeable," passes judgment on mutable and singular existence; the Son links the unchangeable with the changeable in a single person, but this linking is accomplished only by means of another distinct, particular individual; it is the Holy Spirit who effects a joyful reconciliation of the Unhappy Consciousness in an entire community of religious believers.[35] Still these reconciliations in the life of the Trinity are halting and incomplete approximations to the full reconciliation of the Unchangeable with the transitory which will be achieved by

philosophical reflection. This succeeds where the Crusades failed: they engaged in a vast geographic-historic trek to the abode of their "unchangeable Being," but came upon no more than the empty grave of the vanished particularity they sought.[36]

This same empty tomb, "the death of death," represents a step in the dialectical movement of Absolute Spirit. The Resurrection is given a rational interpretation from the perspective of speculative knowledge: it is "this negative of the negative." [37] The Incarnation, the achievement of self-consciousness in man by the divine nature, is "negativity:" Spirit has denied itself by assuming human nature.[38] But the God-man must die in order that he may live—more precisely, that he may rise to universality of life: "Death then ceases to signify what it means directly—the non-existence of *this* individual—and becomes transfigured into the universality of the spirit, which lives in its own communion, dies there daily, and daily rises again." [39] The whole exists for the particular person, and the person is the result of dynamic activities within a community of persons. Hegel writes,

> Morality, love, just mean the giving up of particularity or of the particular and its extension to universality, and so, too, is it with the family and friendship. . . . In Friendship and love I give up my abstract personality, and in this way win it back as concrete personality.
>
> It is just this winning back of personality by the act of absorption, by the being absorbed into the other, which constitutes the true nature of personality.[40]

Richness of personality is the outcome of sharing in a total richness of personality.

Philosophy and Religion

Hegel's idealism affirms the identity of man's act of thinking and what is thought, the identity of man's processes of reflection and God. Through *experience (Erfahrung)* the finite human consciousness attains a self-awareness of truth by which it recognizes itself as spirit, "the whole," or Absolute. The mind mediates itself in a dialectic of estrangement and reconciliation. In the human apprehension of truth Hegel discerns the divine Idea

realizing itself in its unity and internal dialectic. Individual experience is a moment or phase of the universal Spirit. The divine or absolute *Geist* becomes a reality only through man's self-consciousness, i.e., self-awareness. In fact, "God" is nothing other than man's knowledge of God, his "knowing himself in God." [41]

Hegel's philosophy subsumes theology into itself, "Philosophy, therefore only unfolds itself when it unfolds religion, and in unfolding itself it unfolds religion; thus religion and philosophy come to be one. Philosophy is itself, in fact, worship; it is religion, for in the same way it renounces subjective notions and opinions in order to occupy itself with God." [42] Philosophy penetrates and discloses the rationality inherent in the entire process. It is thinking that is man's supreme achievement, and it is philosophical thought that bears the distinction of being the great reconcilor of the real and the rational:

> And here it becomes apparent, too, that philosophy does not stand above its age as if it were something absolutely different from the general character of the time, but that it is One Spirit which pervades both the actual world and philosophical thought, and that this last is only the true self-comprehension of what is actual. Or, in other words, it is one movement upon which both the age and its philosophy are borne, the distinction being only that the character of the time still appears to present itself as accidental, and is not rationally justified, and may thus even stand in an unreconciled, hostile attitude towards the truly essential content; while philosophy as the justification of principles, is at the same time the universal peace-bringer and universal reconciliation.[43]

In philosophical thought the great insights of religion are preserved. Only in what Hegel terms Absolute Religion, i.e., in revealed religion, does the Divine Being achieve self-awareness in man. There spirit knows itself as spirit. [44] Hegel's identification of the content of revealed religion with what one attains through the speculative knowledge of God is disconcerting, yet it is integral to his dialectic of the religious consciousness. The arch-gnostic characteristics of his system are evident here. Actually, however, philosophy supersedes the insight on the part of revealed religion that ultimate reality is spiritual. Christianity confines history too

literally to the unique moment of the God-Man—though within the religious community the particularity of the events in the life of the God-Man give way to the birth of a universal religious consciousness. Philosophy, or what Hegel calls Absolute Knowledge, goes beyond the immediacy of religion, involving "a comprehensive knowledge through notions." [45] The thinking self here rises above the imaginative forms and externals of religion to certainty of truth and a comprehensive awareness of the self as spirit.

The affinity to Boehme becomes clear in the assertion that the dialectic of thought transcends faith. Hegel's philosophy is an attempt to grasp the ultimate absolute identity. Matter and spirit are reconciled by a being combining both. God's revelation in history is identical with the existence of God. In this way Hegel reconciles the transcendent and the immanent. None of our dialecticians so explicitly and systematically transforms faith into knowledge, the shadowy insights of "positive religion" into philosophical insight, as does Hegel. His *gnosis* dissolves all the finite and limited truth of religion into rational intelligibility.

History and Freedom

For Hegel, logic deals with the formal articulation of concepts and the manner in which they are related to one another. However, though the movement of dialectic has its source in logic, in the science of the Idea, it is not confined to logic. The divine Idea develops in history. It adopts successive forms, and proceeds to both transcend and remember its more abstract earlier stages. Human experience is the dynamic unfolding of Spirit: this unfolding of Spirit in time is the encompassing principle that unifies the myriad experiences of the universe. For Spirit is nothing other than "self-contained existence," i.e., one is not dependent on something outside oneself, and this is the definition of Freedom. [46] The individual participates in a reasonable order in full spiritual awareness, and his rights as a person are increasingly protected by social and political institutions.

The unfolding of Spirit is thus nothing distinct from the progressive realization of Freedom, "for the history of the world is nothing but the development of the idea of freedom." [47] Freedom

is realized, in its different forms, through a dialectical unfolding of its moments. Man's "essence" is thus always determined by the freedom he has realized. [48] The freedom that the Oriental world knew, that *one* is free, was far removed from genuine freedom; it expressed itself merely in the anarchy of caprice: the *one* is simply a despot. This generates its opposite among the Greeks and Romans, a democracy and aristocracy in which only *some* are free. Spirit presses on to a new synthesis. The German nations became conscious that man as such is free. [49] The oppositions between external and internal, objective and subjective, human nature and divine nature, this present changing world and the eternal world of the Unchangeable, are overcome, largely through the influences of Christianity. The German peoples become the bearers of the Christian principle, i.e., the principle of spiritual freedom, or reconciliation. [50] The individual now inwardly appropriates to himself and gives his approval to the content of reasonable laws. Hegel emphasizes the rational character of this progression of Spirit in time. It is one of the few philosophies of history which takes so unambiguous a view of progress, yet the centrality of man's freedom in this development imparts a certain grandeur to his sweeping view.

Thus the dialectic of Hegel, all-embracing as it is, explicated in its intricate nuances, is reconciled in the unifying principle of Spirit, or Freedom. The dialectic is provisional in that it describes "moments" in a unified, goal-directed process. Without overlooking Hegel's idealist insistence that "the truth is the Whole," and without denying the limitations of such an isolated judgment in the framework of Hegel's inclusive system, we may nevertheless emphasize Hegel's concern for the particular, concrete person.

For it must be emphasized that the goal of this entire process is for Hegel not some process outside man, but man himself. He emphasized that no single element in the system constitutes the truth, that "the truth is the whole." But he indicates unmistakably, though this is often forgotten, that the freedom of the concrete person is the focus of Spirit, "The highest and acutest point is simple personality, which, by virtue alone of the absolute dialectic which is its nature, equally holds and comprehends everything within itself because it perfectly liberates." [51] Nothing is excluded

from the range of Hegel's dialectic. Its grandeur became the splendor and tragedy of his age. And his various heirs were to seize upon fragments of the "system" to forge quite different types of dialectic.

Notes

1. *Critique of Pure Reason,* tr. J. M. S. Meiklejohn (New York: Willey Book Company, 1943), p. 50.
2. *Ibid.,* p. 51.
3. *Ibid.,* 5, 52.
4. *Ibid.,* pp. 238-62.
5. *The Logic of Hegel,* tr. William Wallace (Oxford: Clarendon Press, 2nd rev. ed., 1892), par 48, p. 83.
6. *Ibid.,* par. 81, pp. 128-9.
7. *Ibid.,* par. 81; pp. 126-28.
8. *Ibid.,* par 81; p. 126.
9. *Ibid.,* p. 122.
10. *Ibid.*
11. Cf. Findley, *Hegel: A Re-Examination* (London: Allen & Unwin. 1958), p. 58 ff.
12. *The Logic of Hegel,* par. 81; p. 125.
13. *Ibid.,* p. 126.
14. *Ibid.,* par. 82; p. 131.
15. Translated from *The Science of Logic* by Walter Kaufmann, *Hegel, Reinterpretation, Texts, and Commentary* (Garden City, N.Y.: Doubleday, 1965), pp. 191-2.
16. *The Science of Logic,* tr. W. H. Johnson & L. G. Struthers (London: Allen & Unwin, 1929), vol. II, p. 67.
17. *Ibid.,* p. 67.
18. *Op cit.,* p. 193.
19. *Op. cit.,* p. 194.
20. *The Science of Logic,* vol. I, p. 94.
21. *Ibid.,* p. 96.
22. *Ibid.,* p. 95.
23. Hegel, *The Phenomenology of Mind,* tr. with introduction and notes by J. B. Baillie, 2nd. ed. (London: Allen & Unwin, 1949), pp. 81-2.
24. *Ibid.,* p. 149.
25. *Ibid.,* p. 219.
26. *Ibid.,* p. 226.
27. *Ibid.,* p. 227.
28. *Ibid.,* p. 233.
29. Cf. Kaufmann, *op. cit.,* pp. 152-3.
30. *The Phenomenology of Mind,* 233.

31. *Ibid.*, p. 244.
32. *Ibid.*, p. 245.
33. *Ibid.*, p. 250.
34. *Ibid.*, p. 252.
35. *Ibid.*, p. 253.
36. *Ibid.*, p. 258.
37. *Lectures on the Philosophy of Religion,* tr. E. B. Speirs and J. Burdon Sanderson (London: Routledge & Kegan Paul, first published 1895, reprinted 1962), III, p. 91.
38. *The Phenomenology of Mind,* p. 775.
39. *Ibid.*, p. 780.
40. *The Philosophy of Religion,* III, pp. 24-5.
41. Hegel, *Encyclopedia of Philosophy,* tr. and annot. Gustav Emil Mueller (New York: Philosophical Library, 1959), par. 465 (564), p. 281.
42. *The Philosophy of Religion,* I., 19-20.
43. *Ibid.*, I, 47.
44. *The Phenomenology of Religion,* II, 772.
45. *Ibid.*, p. 810.
46. Hegel, *Lectures on the Philosophy of History,* tr. J. Sibree (New York: Dover Publications, 1956), p. 17.
47. *Ibid.*, p. 456.
48. Richard McKeon, *Freedom and History* (New York: Noonday Press, 1952), p. 930.
49. *Lectures on the Philosophy of History,* p. 18.
50. *Ibid.*, p. 341.
51. *The Science of Logic,* II, p. 483.

6

VENTURER AT THE BRINKS: KIERKEGAARD AND THE DIALECTIC OF THE SUFFERING SELF

Sören Kierkegaard (1813-55) lived out his life in the provincial capital of Copenhagen, but his dialectic was related to the cosmopolitan practitioners of the art from Plato to Schelling. The probing of the supreme dialectician Socrates impressed him most deeply. In certain respects he was always the Socratic dialectician. He had cut his philosophical teeth on *The Concept of Irony in Socrates* and all of his literary works, particularly the pseudonymous productions, are exercises in dialectical communication. Like Socrates, he laid no claim to possessing the truth; by indirect communication he wished, in the sickly situation of the nineteenth century, to serve merely as a midwife at its birth. Dialectic, he trusted, might enable him to witness in all seriousness to the seriousness of Christ. His dialectic is reminiscent of St. Augustine's powerful contrast between the creatures and the Creator, the conditioned and the Unconditioned, but here the "breach" is radicalized. Here the opposition is between the finite and the infinite, the temporal and Eternal, between bondage and freedom, between despair and faith. But the *locus* of the oppositions is always traced to the existing individual. The churchly heritage from Luther is reflected in the sharp antitheses between guilt and perfection in Christ, between the believer in his solitude and the collective in its inauthenticity.

Speculation versus the Existing Individual

The *animus* for Kierkegaard's dialectical attack on dialectic lay in his revulsion against the pretences of "the system." Hegel's fatal assumption that thinking and being are identical was his initial error. Hegel attempts to pawn off his system of logic as a system of being, as ontology. The real is not identical with the reality of ideas. Like Marx, Kierkegaard did not reject the Hegelian reading of the tradition as dialectical. But how could either Marx or Kierkegaard deepen or extend this all-embracing "system"? Marx seized upon the starting point, Mind, and substituted the solid stuff of Matter, emphasizing a triadic progression from thesis through antithesis to synthesis. Kierkegaard seized upon the oppositions themselves. Hegel obscured the true character of contradictions in reality; he professed to mediate absolute contradictions: "We certainly do not need Hegel to inform us that relative contradictions can be mediated, for it is already told by the ancients, . . . but personality will protest in all eternity against the proposition that absolute contradictions can be mediated (and this protest is incommensurable with the assertion of the mediation), it will in all eternity repeat its immortal dilemma: to be or not to be that is the question (Hamlet)." [1]

Kierkegaard mounts his protest in the name of the existing individual—and in the name of Christian faith. For both personhood and for Christian faith he asserts the need to exist with passionate concern. The concern of Christian faith is identical with that of the rare individual. Both converge at this point in that both affirm contradiction at the heart of man. It could hardly be otherwise for someone who saw the gospel as "communication of existence." Man lives this incredible inner conflict, this excruciating suffering of faith, for "While the understanding is thrown into confusion, faith pushes forth victoriously in the passion of inwardness." [2] The way to truth for the existing individual—and for the Christian—is through the most tortuous inwardness.

In place of Hegel's cognitive or speculative dialectic Kierkegaard insists on an existential dialectic. The individual, irreplaceable, and irreducible reality of the thinker in his subjectivity is the starting point of his dialectic.[3] Hegel achieves his all-embracing

dialectic of thought at the expense of the existential truth of the concrete, existing individual. The passionate, striving, despairing individual is the door to the truth of being. Truth that matters must be subjective truth. It demands passionate concern and commitment from the individual. If he lacks these he deserves to be swallowed up and lost in the dialectic of world history.

Hegel's dialectical process of thought merely alienates man from his authentic individuality. The emotional and polemical vigor of Kierkegaard's attack on what he considered to be a monstrous distortion is clear in his parody: "A thinker erects an immense building, a system which embraces the Whole of existence and world history, etc.—and if we contemplate his personal life, we discover to our astonishment this terrible and ludicrous fact, that he himself personally does not live in this immense high-vaulted palace, but in a barn alongside of it, or in a dog kennel, or at the most in the porter's lodge." [5] A logical system is, indeed, possible. But Hegel was wrong in supposing that he had arrived in his "system" at the truth of being. He had tried to introduce a neglected element, movement, into logic, but Kierkegaard affirms that movement is not attainable via thought but only via the existing subject, the unique individual. This individual must strive—always in existential pathos, in suffering, essentially in guilt—for a truth which is truth *for him*. As a result of the Fall this individual does not have access to the essential state of union with God: his state of existence is at once the actuation and expression of an essential union with God and it is the contradiction of his essential nature. We shall not explore here the dialectical determinants in Kierkegaard's profound analysis of dread. He describes dread as a "sympathetic antipathy and an antipathetic sympathy." [6] One is alarmed while he is captivated, one loves while he fears, for the peculiar object of dread is a "something which is nothing." [7] But precisely here, in the extremities of dread and alienation, can one gain some intimations of what it means to *be*.

Speculation and Faith

Moreover, Hegel had claimed to mediate not in the limited sense that theologians and philosophers had traditionally rec-

onciled contradictory views, much in the manner of Peter Abelard, but he had mediated Christianity and speculation, i.e., Christianity was *explained* from a philosophical point of view; it was transformed into a philosophical doctrine to be elucidated by pure thought; philosophical speculation understood the divine mysteries in a way that faith could never grasp. On the contrary, Kierkegaard says, Christianity is not an idea to be understood but a life lived in faith: "Christianity is the precise opposite of speculation . . . the miraculous, the absurd, a challenge to the individual to exist in it, and not to waste his time by trying to understand it speculatively." [8] Christianity represents a contradiction altogether, forever alien to speculative thought. It is no doctrine that has to be understood, but communication of existence. It is concerned with nothing less than the act of existing, and so it stands at the opposite pole to speculation. It is not something to be grasped intellectually, and thus a phase within speculative thought, as Hegel suggests. There is a vast gulf fixed between knowing what Christianity is—speculatively—and being a Christian.[9]

Men may attempt to exclude something as elusive and inconclusive as dialectic. They may wish to avoid the tortuous course of dialectic and attach themselves firmly and immediately to eternal truth. But Kierkegaard warns:

> Even the most certain of all things, a revelation, becomes *eo ipso* dialectical when I try to appropriate it; even the firmest of things, the infinite negative resolution, the infinite form for God's presence in the individual, becomes immediately dialectical. As soon as I take away the dialectical I become superstitious, and try to swindle God out of each moment's strenuous reacquiring of what has once been acquired.[10]

One must embark upon the difficult and frustrating task of exploring the possibilities of God's disclosing himself in the world of becoming. When one begins to take seriously the very possibility of the eternal revealing himself in the flux of the temporal —to an individual who is himself transformed by such "knowledge"—then he casts off from the safe realm of "historical fact," and launches forth into the uncertainties of historical certainties, i.e., into "objective uncertainty." As long as one remains with the safe niceties of the certainty or reliability of historical facts he un-

derstands nothing of Christian faith. He is still in the realm of "quantitative dialectic" which characterizes all natural science—and history. Kierkegaard sees this dialectic as "approximating, *almost.*"[11] Measurements taken of natural phenomena deal with dimensions and amounts. But in one's relationship to God the ever-more-precise measurements of science contribute nothing but additional confusion. Such measurements obscure the unique situation of the individual before the eternal. Faith does not depend on additional evidence, or on new evidence, but on the qualitative dialectic of faith.[12]

On this Kierkegaard agrees with Lessing that one cannot base his eternal happiness on something historical. Yet Christianity presents itself as an historical religion, rooted in "fact:"

> But now is the historical fact quite certain? To this one must answer: even though it were the most certain of all historical facts it would be of no help, there cannot be any *direct* transition from an historical fact to the foundation upon it of an eternal happiness. That is something qualitatively new.[13]

Kierkegaard expresses little sympathy for the painstaking tasks of historical, linguistic, and archeological research into the beginnings of Christianity. He does not discount such endeavors, but he draws proper attention to the "unspiritual" character of a faith which would calculate so sceptically on the basis of incontrovertible fact. Faith is not the result of weighing counter-probabilities. It is a "qualitative" matter of personal choice, of risk and trial. The offense of Christianity is not something which can be overcome once-and-for-all in an act of faith. Ever and again faith must overcome the scandal to faith. One cannot take refuge in a faith conferred at some point in one's past by the objective sacrament of baptism. Faith is no datum or idea that can be stored and retrieved at will by some kind of computerized data-search, for dialectics requires the inner personal appropriation of the idea: "Every genius, even the stoutest who has ever lived, must utilize with utter singleness of purpose all his strength for the appropriation, the actualization of this inwardness in himself."[14]

The Dialectic of Inwardness

Kierkegaard's conception of the modes of life is a comprehensive presentation of the dialectic of inwardness. He ranks his different "views of existence" according to the proportion of the individual's apprehension of inwardness.[15] These modes, the aesthetic, the ethical, and the religious viewpoints are so many "stances" from which one can live. Each mode is related dialectically to each other, and as natural modes they stand in dialectical relationship to the unique religiousness of Christianity. In *Either/Or* and in *The Stages on Life's Way* he explores variations of the aesthetic mode. They range from the crass sensuousness of Mozart's *Don Juan* to the sophisticated calculations of Johannes the Seducer in *The Stages.* But all alike, as "aesthetes," live for the great moment, the transitory excitement of pleasure. Above all else, one must enjoy himself! The ethical demand of the Eternal has not laid its claim on him, for he has not discovered his existence "before God." He lacks any sense for the continuity or commitment of life; the bond of marriage, so central to the ethical sphere, is avoided like the plague. The aesthete is at home in the distinctive category of "immediacy." [16] Yet this is a questionable immediacy, *"But he who says that he wants to enjoy life always posits a condition which either lies outside the individual or is in the individual in such a way that it is not posited by the individual himself."* [17] The source of the sought-after pleasure lies outside the individual, as in wealth or prestige. Or satisfaction in life is conditioned by the exploitation of some talent. He has not chosen, in all freedom, to be himself.

This stance before the fullness of life is thoroughly undialectical. The dialectic of life is excluded from life: *"Immediacy, the aesthetic,* finds no contradiction in the fact of existing: to exist is one thing, and the contradiction is something different that comes from outside." [18] As the aesthetic individual attempts to maintain or expand the level of enjoyment he fights the increase of boredom and satiety. Such a life contains the seeds of its own dissolution. But since the aesthete lacks a self he is really in despair: he no longer holds out the possibility of raising himself from the morass of such a "choiceless" life. Only by recognizing himself as

a despairing self can he find his true self—in the ethical sphere. But this "transition" from the aesthetic to the ethical is a qualitative change which can only be characterized adequately as a "leap." The aesthetical is not annihilated; it is transfigured. It has been excluded as the absolute to be retained now as the relative.[19] The "moment" is now preserved by being integrated into the flow of a structured life: through the execution of ethical tasks man realizes the self.[20] Here a man "becomes" in contrast to the static and frozen character of the aesthetic sphere. He is transformed through participation in the infinite movement of ethical decision.[21]

The ethical man lives for an ethical ideal. He commits himself to this at a particular time, as in the key relationship of marriage, but this commitment retains its binding force throughout life. In contrast to the evasion of any deep involvement in the aesthetic sphere, free choice stands out here: a man chooses to become himself in continuous realization of freedom in contrast to the aesthete's life of necessity "as part and parcel of the world-process." [22] Entry into the ethical mode is possible only by way of the crisis of choice: only through choosing does one attain personality. The ethical man enjoys a life integrated by a high conception of duty, as Judge William describes this mode in *Either/Or:* "He has clad himself in duty, for him it is the expression of his inmost nature. When he has thus oriented himself he has become absorbed in the ethical and will not chase breathlessly after the fulfillment of his duties. The genuine ethical individual therefore possesses calmness and assurance because he has no duties outside himself but in himself." [23] Such duties do not fragment the self, as do the pleasures of the aesthetic stage, but are integrated in the most intimate fashion into a higher dimension of the self. The ethical man has realized, in his concrete, irreducible circumstances, his unique individuality, and has thus realized in himself universal man.

But there are serious limitations to the ethical sphere. Contradictions present themselves to the ethical man which are simply insurmountable. Clashes emerge between conflicting duties, as between those toward society and family. He faces discrepancies between universal law and the demands of particular situations. Here man's rational faculties are exercised on universal demands

in the form of a code of ethics; but faith entails action enlisting the entire personality. In religious faith the unique individual facing unique situations takes the place of universal rules. The self-sufficiency of the ethical stance is seen, from the way of faith, for what it is, inadequate and delusory. Only when one has died to the world can one return to the world, by faith. Faith lies beyond the dialectic of thought; it is the "power of the absurd," believing "by virtue of the absurd." [24] Abraham, the patriarch of faith, illustrates this passage beyond the sphere of universal moral laws when he is willing to sacrifice the son of God's own promise. Not only Abraham, but anyone who would respond in faith to the absolute duty toward God must do so in solitude, in risk, in fear, and trembling. Kierkegaard himself faced such an agonizing possibility of being mistaken, and so must every man who would forsake the security of the ethical. As persistent struggle and victory characterize the ethical mode so suffering characterizes the religious: ". . . suffering is of crucial importance for a religious existence, and precisely as the mark of inwardness: the more the suffering, the more the religious existence." [25]

But Kierkegaard distinguishes within the religious mode between two distinct dimensions, between Religion A, a religion of immanence, and Religion B, the distinctive Christian religiousness. The former, human religiousness, concentrates self-sufficiently on the spiritual resources within the individual, and for such truth Socrates stands out as its supreme realization. Here truth is subjectivity: it is dependent on personal, inner decision. For Christian religiousness the very opposite holds: subjectivity is the untruth. [26] Truth must be revealed. It enters into history, into human existence: since this is eternal truth juxtaposed with human existence one is dealing with the paradox, and with this the absurdity of faith, "The Absurd is—that the eternal truth has come to be in time, that God has come to be, has been born, has grown up, and so forth, just like any other human being, altogether indistinguishable from other individuals. . . ." [27] With the appearance of this truth in human existence there appears a new sense of sin, a new risk, and a new sense of self. Such a new level of the self is attainable only before God's highest "measure and goal," God's revelation in Jesus Christ:

> A self directly before Christ is a self potentiated by the enormous gift of God, potentiated by the enormous significance which is placed on him by the fact that God, for the sake of this self also, let himself be born, become man, suffered, and died. The greater the apprehension of God, the greater the self; likewise it is true that the greater the apprehension of Christ, the greater the self. That Christ is the measure is a divinely attested expression of the vast reality a self has, for only in Christ is it true that God is man's goal and measure, or measure and goal.[28]

But there is also a new level of dialectic reached when one is dealing with such a breach between the temporal and the eternal: "If the individual is paradoxically dialectical, every remnant of original immanence being destroyed and all connection cut off, the individual being brought to the extremity of existence, then we have the *paradoxical religiousness.*" [29]

The Dialectic of Personal Risk

Thus in place of the Hegelian dialectic of reconciliation of contradictions Kierkegaard posits in his own life, and for every life worthy of the name, the dialectic of contradiction. Yet contradiction does not form the totality of his dialectic. There is also risk. When one faces the brokenness of existence and reaches the limits of one of the existence-spheres he is challenged to choose, to dare, to "leap" to another stage. He must risk the loss of the self to gain a "higher" self. The contradiction is not "mediated" as in Hegel to form a higher stage of unity, but it is nevertheless overcome, in Kierkegaard's distinct sense "annulled" *(aufgehoben),* in the "leap" to the higher mode. Kierkegaard's individual is engaged in the continual dialectic of purifying the self, just as Kierkegaard was continually engaged in the parallel task of purifying the understanding of Christianity. The two are not disjoined: the dialectical analysis of the one is also the purification of the other. The paradoxical religiousness of the Christian stage is a participation in the paradox of Christianity. Neither task was completed by Kierkegaard, nor are they by any man. But he was on his way to becoming an existing individual. He recognized, at least, the possibility, and he chose with uncompromising serious-

ness. He had lived through the various levels, had not cringed before their demands, had ventured to risk their perilous brinks. Through his suffering there emerged in him the synthesis of the temporal and the Eternal. Such an unsteady unity was—and is—available to man in the face of contradictions. Kierkegaard saw as his task the answering of the question "How does one become a Christian in Christendom?" In the face of quintessential suffering and unspeakable joy his "witness" to Christianity was no system of thought or integrated program of action, but a broken life offered in humility, with humor, and with personal risk that has few equals in all of history

Notes

1. *The Journals of Soren Kierkegaard: A Selection,* ed. and tr. Alexander Dru (Oxford University Press, 1938), No. 286.
2. *Afsluttende uvidenskabelig Efterskrift,* Samlede Vaerker, vol. 7 (Copenhagen: Nordisk Forlag, 1925), p. 210n. Translated by David F. Swenson and Walter Lowrie as *Concluding Unscientific Postscript* (Princeton University Press, 1941).
3. Cf. Hermann Diem, *Kierkegaard's Dialectic of Existence* (London: Oliver and Boyd, 1959), p. 21 ff.
4. *Efterskrift,* p. 339.
5. *The Sickness unto Death,* tr. Walter Lowrie (Princeton University Press, 1941), p. 68.
6. *The Concept of Dread,* tr. Walter Lowrie (Princeton University Press, 1946), p. 38.
7. *Ibid.,* p. 39.
8. *Efterskrift,* p. 367.
9. *Ibid.,* 368-9.
10. *Efterskrift,* p. 26n.
11. *The Diary of Søren Kierkegaard,* tr. Gerda M. Andersen, ed. Peter P. Rohde (New York: Philosophical Library, 1960), p. 96.
12. *Ibid.,* 96-7.
13. *The Journals* (Fontana), 184-5.
14. *Efterskrift,* p. 36n.
15. *Ibid.,* p. 562.
16. *Ibid.,* 563.
17. *Either/Or,* II, 152.
18. *Efterskrift,* 563.
19. *Either/Or; A Fragment of Life,* tr. David F. Swenson and Lillian M. Swenson (Princeton University Press, 1944), II, 150, 190, 212.
20. *Ibid.,* 210.

21. *Ibid.*, 189.
22. *Ibid.*, 195.
23. *Ibid.*, 213.
24. *Fear and Trembling,* tr. Robert Payne (New York: Oxford University Press, 1946), p. 36 ff.
25. *Efterskrift,* 275.
26. *Ibid.*, 193 ff.
27. *Ibid.*, 196 ff.
28. *The Sickness unto Death,* p. 186.
29. *Efterskrift,* 562-3.

7

WALKER ON THE NARROW RIDGE: KARL BARTH AND THE DIALECTIC OF THE HUMAN AND DIVINE

Karl Barth (1886-1968) was destroyer and creator, atomizer and synthesizer. His unfinished *summa* is the prodigious achievement of a master dialectician. What was destroyed by the Barth of the *Römerbrief* was the easy harmony in nineteenth century theology between man's religiousness and God's Word. Man's religious capacities remain for Barth, on the level both of thought and action, within the confines of merely *human* potentialities. All human competences, all of man's civilization and culture, particularly his loftiest achievements decked out under a "religious" aura and sanctified by his cultural theologies, are shattered before the stupendous reality of God. Barth's Protean work marks the end of one era and the beginning of another both in the history of Christian thought and the Western Christian heritage. His was the long-delayed "counter-achievement" to the achievement of Friedrich Schleiermacher.[1] The aesthetic versions of religion which sanctified the comfortable bourgeois culture of the nineteenth and twentieth centuries were dissolved. In the carnage of World War I an entire culture had reached the end of its capital, yet it was not bankrupted before its true nemesis, the God of the Bible, who establishes a bond with humanity only in Jesus Christ. Hans Urs

von Balthasar has characterized the first edition of the *Römerbrief*, published in 1919, as marked by, "dynamic eschatology, irrevocable movement from the first aeon of death to the second aeon of divine life, total restoration *(apokatastasis)* of the original ideal creation in God." [2] The movement is from an original identity and immediacy between man and the divine Spirit, through fall into "flesh" (Origen's *katastasis*), to restoration of the spiritual, in a manner and in terms that recall Hegel's Absolute Spirit. A spiritualistic and Platonic anthropology dominates this first edition of the *Römerbrief*. Here the original *identity* of man and God is accented, for man is "particle of the universal divine power." [3] The lost unity in man's relationship to the divine drives to reunion because of "the divine in me," or "the original divine nature in man." [4]

The Second Römerbrief

The famous second edition of the *Römerbrief* published in 1922 sought, in Barth's phrase, to leave no single stone of the first edition in its old lodging.[5] The expressionistic exposition bristles with dialectical oppositions. Negations bristle on page after page, pointing always to God's supreme negation of human possibilities. There is no road from man's religious experience to God: "It is sentimental liberal self-deception to suppose that direct pathways lead in some way from nature and history, from art, morality, science or even religion to the impossible possibility of God." [6] The transition from God's "No" to his "Yes" takes place precisely in the annulment *(Aufhebung)* of this final potentiality. The limits of human presumption must be staked out clearly and concisely.[7] The "No" of God dare never be muffled or set aside, for precisely here is man's hope. And only in God's "No" is there hope. Man's vaunted religiousness is revealed for what it is only in the *krisis* of divine judgment; however, precisely here, in the ruin of everything finite, the infinite is revealed: "He is the hidden abyss, but also the hidden homeland at the beginning and end of all our ways." [8] For in God's "No" to man, his "Yes" is already hidden. Man is drawn into a *krisis* in order that he may experience this divine "No," for since it is complete and since it is *God's* "No" it is also his "Yes." [9] The recognition of this won-

der of justification is no human possibility but is itself a "purely absolute, vertical miracle;" it is "the dialectic of a miracle." [10]

God is the "totally other." The God of the Bible is totally removed from, is the radical opposite of, all of man's petty ideas and subjective feelings regarding the divine. An unbridgeable chasm is set up between sinful man and the transcendent creator-God. Man is "from below," God is "from above." The divine differs totally from every earthly insight by which man may wish to grasp the divine. Man the creature is separated from the Creator-God as sharply as man's understanding, i.e., all his ceaseless questing, is separated from the strange answer which is God. Here Barth restates the Reformed axiom, *"Finitum non capax infiniti."* God and man meet only in the thunderous "No" of God to man's self-satisfied answers. The God of the Bible is infinitely "beyond" the best efforts of man's own cultural and religious life to encapsulate him. In the famous preface to the second edition Barth declared:

> If I have a "system" it consists in the fact that I keep in mind as undeviatingly as possible what Kierkegaard has called the "infinite qualitative difference" between time and eternity, in its negative as well as its positive sense. "God is in heaven and you are on earth." The relation between *this* God and *this* man, the relation between *this* man and *this* God is for me the theme of the Bible and the essence of philosophy in one. Philosophers call this crisis of human knowledge the First Cause. The Bible sees at this crossroad Jesus Christ.[11]

Repudiation of the Analogia Entis

After Kierkegaard's seering critique of Christian religiousness it was still possible for Western man to worship the comfortable idols of his religious aspirations. This man had certainly not been brought to the end of his tether, had not exhausted his well-guarded, though counterfeit religious capital—in order to meet, at long last and *beyond* all human possibilities, that strange divine help which appears only "beyond the limits." [12] Though modern philosophers may still prattle knowingly about some First Cause they are still far from knowing the God of the Bible, who dwells in eternity, in unfathomable darkness, far beyond all the agreeable

analogues known to man. This distant, invisible, and inaccessible God has made himself known on terms which he has chosen, i.e., uniquely in Jesus Christ. In him the "unknown" divine plane meets—in fact, intersects *senkrecht von oben*—the "known" human plane.[13] But here, too, one must be extremely careful if he hopes to glimpse the God who hides himself.

Gustaf Wingren has traced the significance of the basic thesis in Barth's anthropology, "that man lacks the knowledge of God." [14] Reconciliation is restoration of knowledge. This restoration and reconciliation is based significantly, as von Balthasar has emphasized, on the presupposition of original identity.[15] The movement has its source in a lost oneness of man and God still dimly remembered.[16] The process of individuation is pushed to radical antithesis between the human and divine. It attains resolution of this opposition when the "second Adam" annuls the "first Adam:" "The dualism of Adam and Christ, old and new world is not metaphysical but dialectical. It exists only in that it annuls itself *(sich selbst aufhebt)*." [17]

Man's attempt to establish his religion on strictly "rational" or "scientific" grounds was vigorously repudiated by Barth's "No." The word of God is in no way dependent on man's word. It need borrow its rationality from no human sphere. It is dependent on none of the humanistic disciplines, expressions of the human spirit; it bears its rationality and scientific character within itself as God's word. Unbelievers live and think by the inner rationality of God's revelation.[18]

The repudiation of any form of *analogia entis* was a direct corrolary to the dialectic between the human and the divine. If Schleiermacher's theology encapsulated the most fateful aberrations of Protestant thought, Thomistic insistence on analogy enshrined, for Barth, the tragic Catholic error. With regard to the being of man and the unique, peculiar being of God there can be no continuum, only radical disjunction. And at this same point the crucial character of the *Anknüpfungspunkt* for Barth's theology also appears.[19] Emil Brunner simply deluded himself in supposing that he found some points of contact by way of natural theology between the dialectical oppositions. The divine is altogether *divine,* i.e., it is *totally* removed from the all-too-human. And the human

is inescapably human, i.e., it is *totally* devoid of the divine. This world is devoid of God: man is *a-theos,* without God, in an atheistic world. From the standpoint of Barth's antitheses, Brunner was imperfectly dialectical and therefore no crisis theologian. The crisis—a true judgment on a world void of divine vestiges, by a divinity totally other than man—had lost in modern, acommodating theology its qualitative differentia. There is no turning of God to man or of man to God apart from that one divine Word spoken in Jesus Christ. On this same basis Barth derives the law from the Gospel: divine promise precedes command. God's will is revealed wholly and exclusively in God's Word of Christ, the Gospel. The law must be derived "out of" the Gospel and thus the order "Gospel and law" becomes a central feature of Barth's dogmatics.[20] Were Barth to allow a valid knowledge of God and his will through the law he would again be bridging the chasm between the human and divine.

The Dialectic of Reconciliation

The Barth who moved from the second great *Römerbrief* to the *Dogmatics* was no longer the dialectician of opposition. The note of reconciliation sounds forth here in a new and vigorous way. We will not examine the writings of this transitional period from 1922 to 1932, nor will we explore the important *Die christliche Dogmatik im Entwurf* which appeared in 1927.[21] In 1922 Barth himself interpreted his "corrective theology" as no new "*standpoint.*" [22] In view of the infinite distance separating sinful creature and Creator—or, in gradual recognition of this distance, the progressive obliteration of impossible standpoints—just where does man stand? Barth answers that because no standpoint is left for critical modern man dialectical theology calls for a "*mathematical* point," for a "*view*point merely." [23] Since no firm and fixed position remains for any man to speak to God—since at long last it should be clear that no institution, no sacred book, no finite and limited man, can speak with that absolute authority which belongs to the Infinite and Eternal God—man's only resource is the God who reveals himself. The God who is wholly other than man certainly does not reveal himself via the dog-

matism of biblical authority or doctrinal orthodoxy, nor does he reveal himself via the inner voice of mysticism. Mysticism, while criticizing everything human as distinct from the divine, still never ceases to be something altogether human. So mysticism cannot claim to speak of God. Barth then points to the third way, the way of dialectic, which avoids the pitfalls of dogmatism and mysticism yet builds on the insights of both. This way considers man in his most radical and critical, his most basic and pivotal relationship—with God. The dialectician always witnesses to that critical judgment of the divine on the human which reflects God's own "speaking," the unutterable truth that in Jesus Christ this God has become this man. This is beyond the comprehension of any "flatlander," for with regard to the question of God one must always be a dialectician, i.e., a "spacelander:"

> But how now shall the necessary dependence of both sides of the truth upon this living Center be established? The genuine dialectician knows that this Center cannot be apprehended or beheld, and he will not if he can help it allow himself to be drawn into giving direct information about it, knowing that *all* information, whether it be positive or negative, is *not* really information, but always *either* dogma *or* self-criticism. On this narrow ridge of rock one can only walk: if he attempts to stand still, he will fall either to the right or to the left, but fall he must. There remains only to keep walking—an appalling performance for those who are not free from dizziness—looking *from one side to the other,* from positive to negative and from negative to positive.[24]

The cleavage of catastrophic judgment in the *Römerbrief* is replaced in the *Kirchliche Dogmatik* by a new cleaving of human with divine. Barth had repudiated the support of existential philosophy which was operating in the *Christian Dogmatics* of 1927. Human creatureliness and sinfulness, on the one hand, and divine majesty and holiness, on the other, are not merely alien territories. They are still separated by an unbridgeable gulf or chasm. The being and life and act of man are infinitely removed from the being and life and act of God. Man stands in a "No" relationship to God, in opposition, in contradiction, and disruption from God.[25] Between creature and Creator there stands, "a yawn-

ing abyss. Yet this abyss is crossed, not by man, not by both God and man, but only by God." [26] Barth's dialectic, therefore, becomes one of reconciliation, since the synthesis of the human and divine in his Christology becomes the goal of his theology. His anthropology has become an ever more radical Christology. The person of Jesus Christ is the image, the analogue, through which alone man can understand who and what he is. Through his *analogia fidei* Barth accomplishes a basic turning, a placing of man's relation to man in the light of God's revelation of himself.

Barth locates the center of the Christian message, significantly, not in the doctrine of justification, which is merely a single, special phase of reconciliation, but in reconciliation itself. He finds the center in the statement "God with us." God is present in his coexistence with man, making himself known to his people, already in his creation but preeminently in his revelation, i.e., in Jesus Christ. For in Jesus Christ God and man are joined: the antithesis between God and man which has been Barth's abiding theme is overcome in a reconciliation of divine revelation, God's "Yes" to man, which is determinative for Barth's entire system. Yet in this "God with us" there is both acceptance and rejection, for "In the election of Jesus Christ which is the eternal will of God, God has ascribed to man the former; election, salvation, and life; and to himself he has ascribed the latter; reprobation, perdition and death." [27] Christ stands alone in God's rejection on Golgotha, where all men deserve to stand by virtue of their rejection through sin—so that men might stand in his kingdom of life and blessedness. Precisely as the rejected one is Christ the elected. In the place of man, the servant who exalts himself by wanting to become Lord, steps Jesus, the exalted Lord, who humbles himself by becoming a servant. Still Barth rejects any final equipoise between God's dual wills of "Yes" and "No." The "No" of rejection is "overcome" in the "Yes" of God's acceptance. God's acceptance is so inclusive in terms of the Incarnation that there is no exclusion in the predestination of divine grace. All of the contradiction of sin and evil is absorbed in the divine love. A new man is created in Jesus Christ and the old man is destroyed. This old man no longer exists: he has become the new man established in God's life by the divine "Yes." Already in the

present God's promise of forgiveness is given. Man is *totus iustus.*[28]

The dialectic of radical antithesis has eventuated in a dialectic of radical synthesis. Salvation is seen as "participation in the being of God" which takes place in the conjoining of God and man.[29] All men participate in this grace already by creation, but they participate preeminently through the invasion of man's history in the Incarnation.[30] Reconciliation drives through Barth's dialectic with such force—from its source in eternal election through its center in the Incarnation—as to be stopped only in the Origenistic *apokatastasis,* the full restoration of all spirits into harmony with God.[31] The *Kirchliche Dogmatik* can hardly be charged with neglect for man's separation from God by sin and death. Still it is reunion that emerges, beginning with eternal election in Jesus Christ and extending through creation and redemption to the restitution of all things. The *true* and *actual* being of every man is a being reconciled to God, yet only the Christian knows and reflects this being of reconciliation. Only faith discerns, if only dimly, this reconciliation of opposites. The Christian is the example or representative of this new type of existence to those who have not yet experienced it.

However, for Barth this "God with us" means that we know about God: "If the fact that God is with us is a report about the being and life and act of God, then from the very outset it stands in a relationship to our own being and life and acts." [32] Barth writes, "The history of the world which God made in Jesus Christ, and with a view to him, cannot cease to have its center and goal in him. But in the light of this goal and center God cannot say Yes but only No to its corruption." [33] As inaugurator and revealer of "original and essential human existence" Jesus Christ tells us what all men are.[34] There is formal identity and essential disparity, or opposition, between Christ and Adam.[35] The dialectic between human and divine is evident when Barth says of Christ and Adam, "the difference between them is the radical, final, and irrevocable difference between God and man." [36] But there is formal correspondence and identity between them in that both are men, and both as "the one" can represent "the many." [37] So Barth can point, by way of his dialectic, to the more

essential and more significant relationship of man to Christ in contrast to his relation to Adam, "What is *Christian* is secretly but fundamentally identical with what is universally human." [38]

However, the reconciliation in Barth's dialectic does not emerge, as one might expect, from the contradictions themselves. Barth emphasizes again and again that reconciliation appears as a sovereign act of God's freedom.[39] If it flowed from some inner necessity then both God's sovereign freedom and his majesty would be prejudiced. God is in no way bound by the connections he makes.[40] The reconciliation is a theological resolution and not a philosophical operation. The certainty which this conveys to man's knowing surpasses all philosophical knowing. However, whether one develops a philosophy of necessity, as does Hegel, or a theology of freedom, as Barth does, the result is very much the same. Freedom and necessity become, in the words of Jacob Taubes, "amphibolic and ambiguous." [41] The movement of Barth's own dialectic through history simply demands such a harmony of opposites and such a final harmony of all things. A necessity exists for the presence of those who denied the claim of Jesus at the Crucifixion just as there was necessity for those who would affirm him to be the Messiah.

The development of Barth's thought as expressed in the late *Humanity of God* has simply sharpened the focus on reconciliation without adding new structural counterpoise. After forty years Barth proposed, without disclaiming his earlier work, another word about God. He emphasized a neglected *togetherness* of God with man.[42] In Jesus Christ it becomes clear that God's deity "does not exclude, but includes his humanity." [43] Jesus has closed the abyss between God and man, so that God's "No" of condemnation must still be spoken, but it is a "No" that has been displaced by the divine "Yes:"

> However, it must be the "No" which Jesus Christ has taken upon Himself for us men, in order that it may no longer affect us and that we may no longer place ourselves under it. What takes place in God's humanity is, since it includes that "No" in itself, the *affirmation* of man.[44]

God's affirmation of righteousness has broken the validity of his negation of sin, so that man is not under the dialectic of God's

"Yes" and "No" but only under his "Yes." Barth had pointed in this direction much earlier when he emphasized that God's judgment is also an act of his grace.

Man's situation only appears to be contradictory, for in God—and freely in God—a synthesis has taken place. God's final word to man is "Yes," to be displaced by no deeper or complementary "No." The dialectic of Barth, widely read as one of opposition, is really a dialectic of radical reconciliation. Divine affirmation has annulled negation to form a new and sweeping synthesis between the human and divine. Here is no eruption of man's aweful *Dies irae* before a Barthian *rex tremendae majestatis,* only the calm serenity of a harmonious *Agnus dei.* The unapproachable, totally other "creator of heaven and earth" has linked heaven and earth in his own "God with us."

Notes

1. Karl Barth, *From Rousseau to Ritschl* (London: SCM Press LTD, 1959), p. 308.
2. *Karl Barth: Darstellung und Deutung seiner Theologie* (Köln: Jacob Hegner Verlag, 1962), p. 71.
3. Karl Barth, *Der Römerbrief* (Bern, 1919), p. 237.
4. *Ibid.,* pp. 207, 61.
5. Karl Barth, *Der Römerbrief* (München: Chr. Kaiser Verlag, 1922), p. V.
6. *Ibid.,* p. 323.
7. *Ibid.,* p. 226.
8. *Ibid.,* p. 23.
9. *Ibid.,* p. 15.
10. *Ibid.,* p. 37.
11. *Ibid.,* XII.
12. *Ibid.,* p. 226.
13. *Ibid.,* p. 8.
14. *Theology in Conflict* (Philadelphia: Fortress, 1958), p. 28 and *passim.* Cf. CD, IV, 1, 758 ff.
15. *Op. cit.,* p. 77.
16. *Der Römerbrief* (1922), pp. 214, 227.
17. *Ibid.,* 157.
18. Cf. Barth's famous essay on Feuerbach translated in Ludwig Feuerbach, *The Essence of Christianity.* Tr. George Eliot (New York: Harper Torchbooks, 1957), p. 337.
19. Cf. Jacob Taubes, "Dialectic and Analogy," *Journal of Religion,* XXXIV (1954), p. 117.

20. Cf. Karl Barth, *Evangelium und Gesetz* (*Theol. Exist. heute* 32), (1935), 9-12.
21. For such an examination cf. von Balthasar, *Op. cit.,* pp. 93-116.
22. Karl Barth, *The Word of God and the Word of Man.* Tr. Douglas Horton (Boston: Pilgrim Press, 1928), p. 98 ff.
23. *Ibid.*
24. *Ibid.,* p. 206-7.
25. Karl Barth, *Church Dogmatics,* tr. Rev. G. W. Bromiley (Edinburgh: T. and T. Clark, 1936 ff.), IV, 3, 3. Hereinafter cited as CD.
26. CD, IV, 1, 82.
27. CD, II, 2, 162 ff.
28. CD, IV, 1, 596.
29. CD, IV, 1, 8.
30. CD, II, 2, 121.
31. Karl Barth, *The Humanity of God* (Richmond, Va.: John Knox Press, 1960), 61-62.
32. CD, IV, 1, 7.
33. CD, IV, 1, 506.
34. Karl Barth, *Christ and Adam,* tr. T. A. Smail (New York: Collier Books, 1962), p. 41.
35. *Ibid.,* 49.
36. *Ibid.,* 50.
37. *Ibid.,* 114 ff.
38. *Ibid.,* 111.
39. CD, IV, 1, p. 79, and *passim.*
40. *Ibid.*
41. "Theodicy and Theology: A Philosophical Analysis of Karl Barth's Dialectical Theology," *Journal of Religion,* XXXIV (1954), p. 239.
42. Karl Barth, *The Humanity of God,* 45. 1960), 45.
43. *Ibid.,* 49.
44. *Ibid.,* 60.

8

BRIDGE-BUILDER BEYOND THE BOUNDARIES: TILLICH'S DIALECTIC OF ESTRANGEMENT AND RECONCILIATION

The dialectic of Tillich bears marks and acknowledges indebtedness to the long tradition of dialectical thinking from Plato, through Boehme, Schelling, and Hegel, to Marx and Kierkegaard.[1] As a dialectician he is as thoroughgoing as any of these, even culminating their efforts by the inclusiveness and productivity of his dialectical skills. Problems attempted and left unresolved in the tradition are restated and reshaped into new syntheses by Tillich.

The Heritage from Plato and Hegel

Tillich reveals his own dialectical stance when he gives his Platonic definition of dialectic: "Dialectics is the way of seeking for truth by talking with others from different points of view, through 'Yes' and 'No,' until a 'Yes' has been reached which is hardened in the fire of many 'No's' and which unites the elements of truth promoted in the discussion."[2] The Platonic heritage is also apparent in his insistence that the truth of ideas is inescapably relative to the thinker's time and place. The thinker enjoys no perspective on the entire temporal process. He stands, rather, at

a particular moment of qualitatively fulfilled time. There is, therefore, an ambiguous character to all existential knowledge, to all truth. Truth is relative to and normed by the *kairos:* "Dialectics is the attempt to comprehend the fate of the ideas from our Kairos, from the fate of our period."[3]

But Tillich's is not simply a formal dialectic. It is existential: "Dialectics is the art of determining the relation of ideas to one another and to existence. One is led beyond this subjective use of the word dialectics by the reflection that dialectics grasps truth only when the ideas themselves bear a relationship to one another and to existence, to which the dialectic form is suited; in other words: when the ideas themselves are dialectical. Thus, from an art of discovering relationships, dialectics becomes an expression for a certain kind of actual relationship."[4] Life processes of all types, all historical processes, are dialectical, i.e., they drive beyond themselves and return to themselves. They involve conflict and separation; they push toward reconciliation and syntheses, without, however, attaining final syntheses in history. Only in man's personal existence is this drive toward self-transcendence fully actualized.[5] Tillich affirms insights in the dialectic of Hegel as well as of Plato. He distinguishes between an "objective" or "real" dialectic and a "subjective" or "methodological" dialectic:

> Wherever life comes into conflict with itself and drives toward a new stage beyond the conflict, objective or real dialectic takes place. Wherever such processes are described in terms of "yes" and "no," subjective or methodological dialectics are used. The movement of life from self-identity to self-alteration and back to self-identity is the basic scheme of dialectics, and we have seen that it is adequate even for the symbolic description of the divine life.[6]

The fact that man can negate some assertions or that he may be in error in making some assertions points, Tillich asserts, beyond the sphere of logical relationships to the ontological distinction between being and nonbeing. Nonbeing is something more basic to being than any status as a logical concept would indicate: man is that being separated in his existential being from his essential being, and negative or erroneous judgments stem from this dialectical relationship between being and nonbeing:

> What is the structure of this being which is able to transcend the given situation and to fall into error? The answer is that man, who is this being, must be separated from his being in a way which enables him to look at it as something strange and questionable. And such a separation is actual because man participates not only in being but also in nonbeing. Therefore, the very structure which makes negative judgments possible proves the ontological character of nonbeing.[7]

Parmenides tried to evade the participation of nonbeing in being by asserting "Only Being is," but he merely ended in atomism and the failure to account for becoming.

Dialectic in the Trinitarian Life

Like Boehme and Hegel, Tillich locates dialectical movement within both infinite and finite being. The alternative to dialectical movement Tillich sees as a dead identity incapable of accounting for change. The divine life, too, drives toward self-transcendence: it goes out from itself and returns enriched to itself.[8] The three divine principles are moments in a rational process, the process of divine unfolding.[9] The first principle is the inexhaustible *abyss*. It is the power of being resisting nonbeing, the depth dimension of all reality, impermeable by the categories of reason because ontologically inexhaustible. Tillich says of it: "This power of being is the *prius* which precedes all special contents logically and ontologically."[10] Giving meaning and structure to this first principle is the second principle, the *logos*. Through it the divine is rendered "distinguishable, definite, finite."[11] The divine mystery manifests its rational character, but remains a mystery. The third principle is the Spirit, "in whom God 'goes out from' himself, the Spirit proceeds from the divine ground. He gives actuality to that which is potential in the divine ground and 'outspoken' in the divine *logos*. Through the Spirit the divine fullness is posited in the divine life as something definite, and at the same time it is reunited in the divine ground."[12] The self-transcendence of the divine life is completed, like Boehme and Hegel, in the self-transcendence of the entire finite order. The transcendence of

creatures in their finite freedom is identical with the divine self-transcendence in God's infinite freedom.[13] Yet Tillich dissociates himself from pantheism here by emphasizing the reality of finite freedom in the created order—precisely man's freedom and capacity to transcend the self guarantee the transcendence of God.[14]

Existential Estrangement and Essential Unity

But Tillich's systematic theology is an examination of the dialectic of man's existential estrangement and ontological reconciliation. His entire system is an explication of the cleavage between the existential estrangement of life and the essential, or potential, unity of life. The cleavages are discovered and analyzed in man, in the world, and in the divine life. In his freedom man has turned from his essential unity with the creative ground of his being.[15] Yet by his state of being ultimately concerned he participates potentially in the infinite.[16] The manifold ambiguities of life are traced back to this fundamental dialectic within being. Life is always ambiguous precisely because it manifests these existential and essential elements. The dialectic of existential separation and essential unity operates at the very heart of Tillich's theological method, his procedure of correlating questions implicit in the human situation with the answers of the Christian message. Theo-logy itself is inescapably dialectical, i.e., it always mediates between the divine mystery, *theos,* and human understanding, *logos.* Theologies which would fail to be dialectical, i.e., mediating, would fail as theo-logies.[17] Philosophy analyzes the ranges of human existence and isolates those questions which must be answered by revelation, by God as man's ultimate concern.

Tillich himself, by his participation in whole ranges of man's artistic and scientific quests, contributed to the existential analysis of the human predicament—he sharpened the questions. His analysis of man's estranged condition, in which he admits the pioneering explorations of Hegel, stands as one of the most cogent ingredients of his systematics and of his powerful preaching. His success at this point is a testimony to the primal power of his dialectic between essence and existence. One is estranged from that to which one essentially belongs, from that in which one par-

ticipates, though imperfectly. But whereas for Hegel the gap between existential estrangement and essentialist fulfillment is overcome in history through the self-realization of the Absolute, for Tillich the ambiguities remain; the fulfillment promised by the Kingdom of God lies "beyond history" rather than within the historical process. The negativity present in human existence is never removed—only in God is the split between essence and existence transcended in perfect being, i.e., the divine life is unambiguous because it is not disrupted by existential estrangement

The transition from essence to existence is symbolized by Adam, representing sin as universal fact and as free act, the figure for individual freedom and collective destiny.[18] Tillich examines the operation of this dialectic more specifically in terms of key "polar elements of being:" freedom in conflict with destiny, dynamics in its struggle with form, individualization in estrangement from participation.[19] Over against the determinism of Hegel, Tillich emphasizes the role of human freedom, of free decision within a community of persons. Freedom may be distorted by *hubris* or concupiscence and thus miss an appointment with destiny.[20] Destiny offers man a limited number of live options, it is not sheer mechanical automatism; it rather demands the risk of appropriate decision in specific moral acts.[21] The result is a true dialectic of freedom-joined-to-destiny; essential possibilities are actualized in a process by which the self transcends itself. The process embraces distinguishable elements—morality, culture, and religion, all in the inseparable unity of the spirit. Tillich explores the dialectic present in the disruption of dynamics and form. Dynamics requires form—in the essential condition of man they are united. But continually dynamics shatters form and the result is chaos. Or form stifles vital force and the result is rigidity.[23] Dynamics and form are always interdependent: old forms are shattered, giving rise to chaos, and new forms emerge. Creative emergence of new forms is always coupled with the destruction of the old; even in the divine depths this dialectic of self-creativity and self-destruction is reflected.[24] Life requires the movement of self-integration between the centered self and the manifold elements surrounding it.[25] Within existential estrangement this

process of attaining balance through integration and experiencing disruption through disintegration always goes on.[26] Self-identity is always coupled with self-transcendence in all processes of life.

Another dialectic within man's estranged condition is that between individualized being and participation. In order to "be" as particular beings all forms of life must be individualized, yet in order to "be" they must participate in the unity of being. Individualization reaches to the extremes of loneliness and depersonalization in the more destructive forms of estrangement: man is deprived of participation in being. But individualization may also be inadequate and in such instances participation, too, remains minimal. The false individualization of the collective represents both the lack of individual being and failure to participate.[27] In each of these polarities Tillich sees a genuine dialectic of separation and reunion taking place.

The Dialectic of Despair and Faith

Tillich has been able to apply his analysis of estrangement in a powerful way to psychological problems. Man's existential situation is one of despair. It is at the utmost depths of despair, when the presence of the divine is in total eclipse before doubt and meaninglessness, that the "courage of despair" appears. The more devastating the corrosion of doubt the more dynamic is the power of faith to overcome such doubt. The acceptance of this despair is itself faith. The soundly dialectical reason for this, Tillich declares, is that an affirmation is implicit in a negation.[28] Despair is a vital action; as such it can never be *simply* negation. But here Tillich takes no leap from despair into the acceptance of a set of eternal verities or some guaranteeing authority; the state of despair, essentially the awareness of being finite, cannot be set aside by such false solutions. One must affirm his acceptance by the power of being-itself, by "the infinite ground of courage." [29] The faith that does this is not directed toward the personal God of traditional theism. It is "absolute faith," with "no special content." [30] It is the courage to accept one's acceptance *in spite of* estrangement, sin, and despair. It is the perception of meaning within meaninglessness.

But the spanning of these tensions by faith involves taking a chance. It entails risk, for it places the center of personality in what may prove empty. One affirms the self out of the depths of radical doubt. Thus doubt does not stand at the opposite pole from faith but is a constituent of faith. Tillich says: "Courage participates in the self-affirmation of being-itself, it participates in the power of being which prevails against nonbeing." [31] The divine is not something distinct from man, no "supernatural" being standing over against man, but is to be found precisely in the world, in the depths, as "being-itself." In his acts of courage man simply participates in the power of being which conquers non-being. Such acts have revelatory significance: the inexhaustible depths of human existence are manifested to the religious consciousness. They become "a key to an idea of God which transcends both mysticism and the person-to-person encounter." [32]

The Power of Being Resisting Nonbeing

Here, again, Tillich is employing his method of correlation: he correlates the ambiguities of estranged, i.e., human existence, with being-itself, with the unambiguous, reconciled ground of all being. The questions themselves determine the shape of the answers, "However, if the notion of God appears in systematic theology in correlation with the threat of nonbeing which is implied in existence, God must be called the infinite power of being which resists the threat of nonbeing." [33] The threat of nonbeing in all things—including the state of human despair—is the negative side to the mystery of being. This negative side reveals the "abysmal element in the ground of being." [34] The positive side of the same mystery reveals itself as the divine ground, the power of being.[35] It is this threat posed by nonbeing that drives being to overcome the "No" to itself by saying "Yes" to itself, and thus to transcend itself.[36] Nonbeing is not distant from or distinct from being but is the quality within being itself which continuously negates being. All finite being includes such nonbeing, and God, too, symbolically speaking, as power of being affirms his self as infinite being over against infinite nonbeing. Thus "the anxiety of finitude" is not set apart from the divine blessedness

but stands in a dialectical relationship to infinite or unconditional being.

Reconciliation in the New Being and Kingdom of God

The estrangement of man in the modern world was focused in the apocalyptic counter-passions of two World Wars. It was focused in the self-destructiveness of man, in his perilous harmony with nature, in his failure to manage technical reason. Estrangement has been both focused and universalized for modern man. But over against the profound estrangement experienced by modern man stands love, the dynamic reunion of that which is separated. It is in the experience of love that man overcomes his separation from life, "Love is the source of grace. Love accepts that which is unacceptable and love renews the old being so that it becomes a new being." [37] The dynamics of being requires recognition of separation as well as reunion, for being "separates itself from itself and reunites itself with itself." [38]

Reuniting love reached its supreme expression in the cross of Christ. Here grace was supremely manifested as the acceptance of what is rejected.[39] In one man the separation between essence and existence was overcome: "The paradox of the Christian message is that in *one* personal life essential manhood has appeared under the conditions of existence without being conquered by them." [40] Jesus, too, was torn by the anguish of rejection; he participated in existential estrangement. He struggled with insecurity; he felt the destructive powers of estrangement as the rejected and crucified Messiah. He was open to error and was involved in tragic guilt by rendering his enemies guilty.[41] But by conquering the powers of estrangement and by taking the negativities of existence into his unbroken unity with the Father, Jesus became the bearer of the New Being, the "restorative principle" in Tillich's dialectic.[42] He became the basic sacramental reality, the power to overcome the contradictions of existence. As the Christ he did not lift man out of historical existence, but transformed this existence. He transformed it ultimately, i.e., in Jesus the Kingdom of God was present. Just as "power of being" within God points to the power of being to resist nonbeing, so "New

Being" refers to the power in Jesus to resist the forces of estrangement.[43] Here the gap between essence and existence is closed: here unambiguous life appears. But wherever healing and saving power is at work, i.e., among all men, since they participate in being, there the power of the New Being is manifested. As Satan represents the distorting principle in existence so the Christ represents the positive principle in the New Being.[44]

However, every historical synthesis remains fragmentary and ambiguous. Fulfillment, both within history and beyond history, is represented in the symbol "Kingdom of God." Yet because this points to an "already" of fulfillment of the kingdom in each moment of history and a "not yet," pointing to consummation beyond history, this unifying symbol underscores the abiding cleavage between essence and existence in Tillich's system. Only beyond history will essence and existence be identical, but participation in the reality of the New Being in the present imparts a unity and direction toward the ultimate.[45] Fulfillment of individual life involves participation in the fulfillment of the Kingdom of God. Thus universal estrangement points, for Tillich, to its counterpart "universal essentialization." [46] Tillich's dialectic is thus universal, and reconciliation is completed only beyond history. The positive is at work within existence always overcoming the negative. Each individual life becomes a stage for these positive-negative forces, since "every human being turns against his *telos,* against Eternal Life, at the same time that he aspires to it." [47]

It is difficult to challenge the dialectic of Tillich once given his ontological presuppositions. No doubt it is these presuppositions which require examination. In his ecstatic or self-transcending naturalism the Creator of the world becomes a function of this world, progressively reconciling the cleavages between existential and essential being. It appears that one has the choice of understanding the Creator as radically different from and "other than" this world—with Kierkegaard and the Barth of the second *Römerbrief*—or of seeing Being-itself within man and the world as the source of reintegration—with Boehme, Hegel, and Tillich. The operation of the dialectic in each alternative follows from this prior decision on the relation between Creator and world. Tillich's dialectic of accepting acceptance in spite of one's unacceptability

appears as sheer accommodation to an inevitable fate if one emphasizes with Kierkegaard the need for radical transformation in man worked by a Creator essentially different from his creatures. The radical nature of man's redemption in the biblical perspective may simply be obviated by Tillich's earlier, key decision to identify the Creator-God with Being-itself.

Notes

1. For an evaluation of Tillich's relation to the dialectical tradition see James Luther Adams, "Tillich's Interpretation of History," *The Theology of Paul Tillich,* ed. Charles W. Kegley and Robert W. Bretall (New York: Macmillan, 1952), 294-309.
2. Paul Tillich, *The Protestant Era,* trans. James Luther Adams (Chicago: University of Chicago Press, 1948), p. xiii.
3. "Kairos and Logos," *The Interpretation of History,* tr. N. A. Rasetzki and Elsa L. Talmey (New York: Charles Scribner's Sons, 1936), p. 168.
4. *Ibid.,* 164-65.
5. Paul Tillich, *Systematic Theology,* I (Chicago: University of Chicago Press, 1951), 169 ff.
6. *Systematic Theology,* III (Chicago: University of Chicago Press, 1963), 329.
7. *Systematic Theology,* I, 187.
8. *Ibid.,* 234.
9. *Ibid.,* 25.
10. Paul Tillich, *Theology of Culture.* Ed. Robert C. Kimball (New York: Oxford University Press, 1959), 25.
11. *Systematic Theology,* I, 251.
12. *Ibid.*
13. *Systematic Theology,* II (Chicago: University of Chicago Press, 1957), 8.
14. *Ibid.*
15. *Systematic Theology,* II, 8.
16. *Ibid.,* 9.
17. *The Protestant Era, ibid.*
18. *Systematic Theology,* II, 56.
19. *Ibid.,* 62-6.
20. *Ibid.,* 62 ff.
21. *Systematic Theology,* III, 43.
22. *Ibid.,* 95.
23. *Systematic Theology,* II, 64-5.
24. *Systematic Theology,* III, 51.
25. *Ibid.,* 33 ff.
26. *Ibid.,* 41.
27. *Systematic Theology,* II, 65-6.

28. *The Courage to Be* (New Haven: Yale University Press, 1952), pp. 175-6.
29. *Systematic Theology,* I, p. 64.
30. *The Courage to Be,* p. 176.
31. *Ibid.,* 181.
32. *Ibid.,* 178.
33. *Systematic Theology,* I, 64.
34. *Ibid.,* 110.
35. *Ibid.*
36. *The Courage to Be,* p. 180.
37. *Theology of Culture,* p. 145.
38. Paul Tillich, *Love, Power and Justice* (New York: Oxford University Press, 1954), p. 49.
39. Paul Tillich, *The Shaking of the Foundations* (New York: Charles Scribner's Sons, 1948), p. 147.
40. *Systematic Theology,* II, 94.
41. *Ibid.,* 133.
42. *Ibid.,* 119.
43. *Ibid.,* 125.
44. *Systematic Theology,* II, 171.
45. *Systematic Theology,* III, 270.
46. *Ibid.,* 408.
47. *Ibid.,* 406.

9

WANDERER IN THE FOREST: HEIDEGGER ON THE BEING OF BEINGS

The thinking of Martin Heidegger (1889—) has been dedicated to opening a path. He has sought to open a path to thinking. His massive *Sein und Zeit* (*Being and Time*), first published in 1927, he describes as simply *"unterwegs,"* "on the way." [1] It is devoted to the quest for the meaning of Being, for Being has long since fallen into oblivion. Because of the dialectic in Heidegger's own fundamental ontology and because of the influence he has exerted in recent Christian thought—both as existentialist and as ontologist—it will be well for us to look at the new directions his dialectic has opened for contemporary philosophy and theology.

Heidegger's penetrating analysis of the structures of human existence in *Being and Time* has caused him to be classified as an existentialist more frequently than an ontologist. Still his analysis of these *existentialia,* the fundamental modes of existence of the person, only serves as a key to the nature of Being. It stands in the service of his overarching interest, that of a fundamental ontology, the quest for the meaning of Being. He has sought a setting for the disclosure of Being. Man's situation must be seen from the perspective of his "Being-in-the-world." He cannot be understood, as Western philosophy has persistently tried to approach him, as some isolated subject confronting some equally

isolated object. Man and world are inextricably bound up with one another. Neither may be confused with the other—nor can one be understood apart from the other, for man is inevitably, inextricably related to other beings. Man has the peculiarity of always making use of things around him as tools and he shares his existence in solicitude for others.[2] Heidegger sees "Being-with" *(Mitsein)* as constitutive for man's "Being-there" *(Dasein):* just as man characteristically utilizes things as tools so he is always, inevitably related to others. These others are bound up with his own irreplaceable existence.[3] As we shall see on a moment, *Dasein* is used by Heidegger in a very special way. But we might note at this point that it always points to that unique Being of man which causes him to be concerned with Being. It is no lifeless "what", but always possibility to be itself or not itself.[4]

The Being of Beings

Being is, indeed, still hidden in all the explorations of ontology and metaphysics since Aristotle. Ever and again some particular aspect of that-which-is has been mistaken for Being itself. And not only has Greek philosophy been distorted by this misconception but the God of Christian theology, too, bears all the marks of this confusion of being with some inner-worldly reality. From Aristotle through Descartes and Kant to its culmination in Hegel and its end in Nietzsche, metaphysics has confined itself to that-which-is. It has thought only about beings as beings *(das Seiende als das Seiende)*. But here it is Being *(Sein)* that has manifested itself, has entered a state of unhiddenness to *Dasein*. The roots of metaphysics are planted in a ground which is the truth of Being.[5] Being "resides" or "takes place" *(west)*. It discloses itself in beings and all beings "speak" of their common ground, Being. Being is the Being of beings *(das Sein des Seiendes);* beings occur only in Being. What Heidegger undertakes is thus a Copernican revolution in philosophy, the reorientation of the entire metaphysical tradition from Plato to Nietzsche.

The term Heidegger has chosen for the sphere of Being proper to man is *Dasein* ("being-there"). The term is used in a technical sense to indicate both the involvement of Being *(Sein)* in the

nature of man and man's essential relationship to the "openness," *Da,* the "there" of Being.[6] It is in *Dasein* that the truth of Being reveals itself. Here it is that "Being itself reveals and hides itself, yields itself and withdraws." [7] Somehow, this "there" of man must be the locus of a peculiar unhiddenness of Being, different from the hiddenness of snails and stones. And Being alone, by giving itself to man, can make him free, i.e., make him authentically what he is.

Dasein must be understood in terms of possibilities; this is the remarkable thing about man, that he is potentiality-for-Being. Every *Dasein* has the possibility to be either authentic or inauthentic. As inauthentic man stands before false concerns. Heidegger says of this inauthenticity: "Inauthenticity has the possibility of authenticity as its basis. Inauthenticity characterizes a kind of Being into which *Dasein* can divert itself and, for the most part, also has always diverted itself. Yet *Dasein* does not necessarily and constantly have to divert itself into this kind of Being." [8] *Dasein* is authentic when it is aware of its being-as-possibility. But no one escapes the scattering of vital energy which forgetfulness of Being entails. Inevitably one lives inauthentically, one is in flight from the self; yet inevitably man is also free—a dialectic of enslavement and freedom runs through every personal life. Men permit their possibilities of Being to be snatched away by the always-indefinite "others." The condition chosen by man in inauthenticity is characterized by *Verfallenheit,* fallenness; man is scattered in *das Man,* the impersonal public, and engulfed by *Besorgen,* momentary concerns. In his classic description of this levelling, this concern with "averageness" of the "they" Heidegger writes:

> The "they" has its own ways to be. . . . Every sort of priority is noiselessly suppressed. Overnight everything primordial gets glossed over as something long since well-known. Everything attained by struggle becomes something to be manipulated. Every secret loses its power. This care of averageness reveals again an essential tendency of *Dasein* which we term the "levelling" *(Einebnung)* of all possibilities of Being.[9]

Dasein that has dispersed into the they-self has not yet found itself and is inauthentic. It has not come to grips in dread with

the ultimate possibility of its own being—personal finitude or death. Death is seen as some vague and distant "something" with no bearing on everyday life. A man who loses himself in the "they" or "momentary concerns" lacks the freedom which comes with the acceptance of dread, with acceptance of death; he has not formed that final detachment—from his pitiful attachment to material things—which authentic selfhood requires. Only the acceptance of death, chosen with resolve and open to the fundamental insecurity of existence, leads to freedom. Resolve to death is the condition for human freedom.

Care *(Sorge)* occupies a role for the early Heidegger comparable to *Qual* in Boehme and *Angst* in Kierkegaard. It is for Heidegger the ontological structure of *Dasein:* the inner being of *Dasein* is Care. Man "cares" or is concerned for things, for his world, and so imparts meaning to them. Through this care Being comes to pass. Man experiences his relation to the world as *Geworfensein,* as being thrown into the world. He experiences himself as a stranger cast into a world alien to him. He never escapes this movement of "thrownness." He is always prey to the world, wandering homeless in the inauthentic realms of the "public." Violence is being done to man simply by his painful exile in the world.

Only when concealments and obscurities have been cleared away does *Dasein* disclose to itself, "dis-cover" its own authentic Being. It has shattered its many pretenses.[10] *"Das Man,"* the "one like many," becomes an *"Ich,"* one's own "self." The *Selbstsein,* "Self-being," rather than being completely distinct from *"das Man"* stands in a dialectical relationship to the mode of *"das Man."* One can plan for the future in an inauthentic manner and thus in fact live in the present. Such a man does not really see the primacy of the future as a future. For man in his *Verfallenheit* the future is always viewed as a kind of present: he plans for tomorrow because it will be present, he will be hungry, or he will need money. But the future (for-the-sake-of, *umwillen*) is that which will never be present; it is the anticipation of *Dasein's* unique possibilities in unity with its own distinct "having been."[11] Heidegger emphasizes, in connection with man's choice of authenticity, that this is a *free* choice and it is therefore also a *re-*

sponsible choice. The authentic self makes resolute choices among the many different possibilities of his future. The voice of conscience appears in anxiety, making man uneasy in his inauthentic way of being. It discloses man to himself. It calls man in his fallenness into the world of things, where he relates himself solely to things, and into the depersonalized mass, where he surrenders his own responsibility. It redirects him to look for authentic Being, for the common ground of all beings, for his distinctive possibilities. As Heidegger says, "Conscience calls the Self of *Dasein* from its lostness in the 'they.' "[12] Conscience calls one to resolve to be himself, not to lose himself in deadening routine or mechanical activities. But it is only when *Entschlossenheit* (resolve) takes over in the face of the erasure of any and all meaning by death that one projects oneself onto his original possibilities. One does not know explicitly the possibilities upon which he projects himself. Yet resolve refuses to permit historical necessity to establish any one-sided sway over human life. Man resolves to *be* oneself in dialectical tension with the inescapable forfeiture of self.

Philosophy and Theology

When Heidegger asks the "basic question of metaphysics" in his *Introduction to Metaphysics*, "Why is there any being at all and not rather nothing," both the question and the answer point to an unfolding rather than to the *creatio ex nihilo* of the Christian tradition. The question reveals both a profoundly dialectical ontology and a supremely Gnostic quest. The "nothing" from which beings emerge and which for Heidegger forms the alternative to τό ὄν is evidently the dialectical μη ὄν of Boehme and Hegel. To ask this question, says Heidegger, is simply "foolishness" from the standpoint of Christian faith. The foolishness of philosophy's basic question implicates all philosophy as foolishness. But the answer of Christian faith which renders philosophy a foolishness, the reply that there are beings rather than nothing because God created them, is simply "foolishness" to philosophy. Faith is a "foolishness" because it deflects the philosopher from "this daring attempt to fathom this unfathomable question."[13] Theology is discontent with philosophy's question about "being qua being," and phil-

osophy is dissatisfied with theology's asking about being as creation, i.e., philosophy suspects that Being is seen in Christian theology as *a* being. Both admit that the subject of their inquiry is a mystery, yet both nevertheless pursue their quest, which to the other is a misdirected questing. In 1949, in his introduction to the fifth edition of his lecture *Was ist Metaphysic?* Heidegger asks pointedly, "Will Christian theology some day decide to take seriously the word of the Apostle and thus also regard philosophy as foolishness?" [14]

Being and Nothingness

Heidegger's understanding of "Nothingness" is closely related to the *Nichts* of Boehme. For both it is a primordial and fundamental working It is found in Being itself rather than outside it. It gives rise through primordial discord to Being. But Heidegger develops his dialectic far beyond anything suggested by Boehme when he relates *Dasein* to *das Nichts. Dasein* is suspended in dread *(Angst)* over *No-Thing.* Here Heidegger develops Kierkegaard's analysis of the concept of dread. In dread what-is-in-totality slides away from us. [15] But what is more, we slide or slip away from ourselves. It is in the experience of dread, from the horrible perspective of naked terror into which man is plunged before the abyss of nothingness, that *Dasein* is brought to confront beings *(das Seiende)* as such. [16] Precisely then, in the "clear night of the Nothingness of dread," when the all-too-familiar things of the world uncannily withdraw and we withdraw from our own selves, the attention of *Dasein* is riveted in a new openness on the primal presence of what-is, on beings. [17] They are illuminated in this limit situation as beings rather than as their alternative, Nothingness. These things now stand out in their utter derivative and dependent character. Nothingness reveals beings, for as the "Other" of beings *das Nichts* is the veil of Being.[18] Heidegger says, *"Im Sein des Seiendes geschieht das Nichten des Nichts."* ("In the Being of beings the nihilation of Nothingness occurs"). [19] The nihilation of Nothingness rips aside the veil of everydayness that hides beings from us—and the Being of these beings is experienced as Nothingness. Only when *Dasein* arrives at this point can

Being unveil itself. In the later Heidegger one surrenders to Being. The emphasis is no longer on dread. Being freely gives itself.

Heidegger's profoundly dialectical conception of Being is revealed here in his assertion that *"Das Nichts selbst nichtet"* ("Nothing nihilates itself.") [20] *Nothingness or nihilation*— not annihilation—is present in all beings and is the essence of Being itself. It is the dynamic power of Being that gives rise to Being. Being is not the totality of beings *(das Seiende);* from the perspective of this totality *(das Seiende im Ganzen)* Being *(das Sein)* is a naught *(Nichts)*. Being itself appears as a nothingness. For the coming-into-Presence of Being, for Being's un-concealment, Nothingness is required. In the "letting-be" of beings, Being must simultaneously extend and withdraw; it enters into beings, but by revealing itself thus in beings it conceals itself as Being. This is the self-negation described symbolically as non-Being, the dialectical counterpart to the Presence of Being.

To this hiddenness of nihilation within Being Heidegger traces the "Nay-saying" of negation in reflective thinking. *Das Nichts* takes precedence to all "Nay-saying." [21] All negation in speech and in experience, Heidegger says in his *Letter on Humanism,* is a functioning of nothingness, "The question remains, given that thinking belongs to ex-sistence, whether all 'Yes' and 'No' is not already ex-sistent in the truth of Being. If this is so, then 'Yes' and 'No' are in themselves already bound to Being. As bound to this, they could never first posit that to which they themselves belong." [22]

Being and Thinking

The later Heidegger has emphasized the distinctive role played by man's thinking in the unveiling of Being. The truth of Being occurs in essential thinking, not in representational or logical thinking. In their original coherence this was expressed by Parmenides when he declared "Thinking and Being are the same." [23] Man and Being belong to one another, are present to one another, in common con-cern *(Er-eignis)*. [24] In this connection Heidegger points to the creative thinkers, poets, and statesmen: they are those who give rise to beings by sustaining the original conflict. They serve to build and preserve the world of *physis*.[25] Truth

emerges *from (a-) concealment (-lethe);* it is the "un-concealment" (ἀ-λήθεια) of what is. What is, reality, gives itself to the subject. Should the subject try, in the usual view of thinking, to impose his own categories upon the objects of thought it would obscure rather than unveil itself. Truth, according to Plato's description, must be wrested from its hiddenness.[26] In fact, it is a perpetual wrenching away from a certain hiddenness, ". . . the unhidden steadily overcomes a hiddenness of the hidden. The unhidden must be torn from a hiddenness, must in a certain sense be stolen from this."[27] Thus *a-letheia* is always evaluated in a positive as well as a privative sense: Being itself must be questioned along with the questioning of beings. Heidegger also finds in Plato the beginning of another fateful conception of truth which became decisive in the Western tradition: truth as correctness is oriented to the Idea. Being was seen as an Idea (ἰδέα), *a* being to be correctly viewed (ἰδεῖν) by a spectator. Truth consisted, then, of a conformity between knowing subject and known object. The entire history of truth as *veritas* and the Medieval view of truth as *adaequatio intellectus ad rem,* the correspondence of the intellect to the thing (beings), Heidegger connects with this development. This view resulted in a vast amount of control being achieved over things in the modern age through science and technology, but much of this at least was secured at the immense cost of the forgetfulness of Being.

What Heidegger appeals to is *a-thinking-that-recalls (das andenkende Denken),* a thinking which recognizes the encompassing of the individual by *Being.* Man is uniquely that being in whom Being reveals itself. This occurs in Being, when Being unveils itself via *Dasein's* distinctive awareness—different from that of the things that are. "Thinking," he says in his 1947 *Letter on Humanism,* "brings to fulfillment the relation of Being to the essence of man. It does not create or produce this relationship. Thinking simply offers it to Being as that which has been delivered to it from Being. This offering consists in this, that in thinking Being enters into language. Language is the house of Being. In this dwelling man abides. Those who think and those who create in poetry are the guardians of this dwelling."[28] They let Being be —and thereby share in the lighting-up of the beings. For the most

part, however, language is not recognized and honored as such a dwelling. It is prostituted as an instrument for acquiring domination over beings *(das Seiende).* [29] Heidegger speaks here of a thinking which is basic and primal rather than representational, like the thinking of metaphysics and science. Being is antecedent to thinking; it is no product of thinking; but essential thinking, a thinking which experiences the truth of Being, is an occurrence of Being. [30]

Such thinking which examines the ground of metaphysics has the capacity to effect no less than a transformation in the nature of man. Being might, out of this involvement with man, "generate a radiance which might lead man to belong to Being." [31] Man in the modern age, however, has experienced the absence of Being. He has been abandoned, forsaken to exclusive concern for beings, without becoming aware of his forsakenness.[32] This has, indeed happened to man, who in his essence is claimed by Being. [33] Heidegger calls for a different kind of thinking, a thinking responsive to Being and brought to pass by Being, to overcome our forgetfulness of Being.

The Dialectic of Homecoming and Homelessness

In the *Letter on Humanism* the dialectic of not-being-at-home in the world is set forth most clearly. Precisely by living one "dwells," he dwells in closeness to Being. Man is on the way to Being which transcends him. He approaches the clearing *(Lichtung)* of the forest. When entering the clearing he senses for a brief instant the forest receding. Being unconceals the beings in the forest's darkness, but just as quickly the forest surrounds him again. But it is man who "stands-out" in the clearing of Being. This is "ex-sistence" *(Ek-sistenz).* He "stands out" in openness to Being; freedom grants itself to man, but then again and again he loses himself in the underbrush of forgetfulness in the everyday. Or, from another perspective, Being gives itself and at the same time negates itself in a profound dialectic of revealing and hiding. [34] Thus the lines from Hölderlin's poem *Heimkunft, (Homecoming),* are interpreted as hailing a presence at once veiled and unveiling, "Near and hard to grasp are the gods." One participates

in and yet is estranged from the holy. In our homelessness we wait upon the treasure we have ourselves abandoned. We wander about and form attachments to beings because of our forgetfulness of Being. Our forgetfulness of Being, however, corresponds to the peculiar concealment of the Holy in our time.

In his later works Heidegger has attempted to set forth with new clarity and integrity the disclosure of that-which-regions. In the *Gelassenheit* (translated as *Discourse on Thinking*) he analyses meditative thinking as the key to Being. Even in the world of technology, which depends on calculative thinking, there is a hidden meaning, which continually reveals and hides itself, so that "we stand at once within the realm of that which hides itself from us, yet hides itself precisely in approaching us." [35] What is required is a new kind of thinking, a "letting-be" *(Gelassenheit)* of things and an openness to the mystery. [36] He suggests, "Then thinking would be a coming-into-nearness of distance." [37] Here the dialectical movements of both contradiction and the overcoming of contradiction are symbolized. Meditative thinking, responsive to Being, has the aspect of both bringing near and making far. Man is appropriated by that-which-regions—and he is not, so that the scientist in the conversation can say, "Again we have this restless to and fro between Yes and No." [38] Man "waits upon"—with no object in view—Being which transcends him. [39]

Has Heidegger succeeded in pointing to a path where so many have gone astray? Has he succeeded in delineating a fundamental ontology—and thus in redirecting the course of onto-theological thinking since Plato? Heidegger's thought has been the most creative and productive for theology of any of our contemporaries. The availability of his later thought for theology has only recently received serious consideration. [40] It poses complex problems. There are limitations in his view of man and the world. E.g., man is still viewed in an isolated fashion when seen in his *"Sein zum Tode"* (being-toward-death). Man is also hardly that "stranger" in the world which Heidegger's *gnosis* pictures him to be. Moreover, the New Testament requires a far more drastic conversion through divine grace than Heidegger's privileged illumination entails. On the other hand, Heidegger's dialectical conception of man brings out factors which have been neglected in the Christian view. The

provocative nature of his analysis has belatedly led to a fruitful confrontation with his thought. We may hope that the creative exchange has only begun, that more serious efforts will be made to assess the availability of Heidegger's thought for constructive theology.

Notes

1. *Was ist Metaphysik?* 7th ed. (Klostermann: Frankfurt a.M., 1955), 13.
2. Cf. *Sein und Zeit* 6th ed. (Tübingen: Max Niemeyer, 1949), pp. 120-27.
3. *Ibid.*, 124.
4. *Ibid.*, 12.
5. *Was ist Metaphysik?*, 7-8.
6. *Ibid.*, 13-14.
7. *Ibid.*, 15.
8. *Sein und Zeit*, 259.
9. *Ibid.*, 127.
10. *Ibid.*, 129.
11. *Ibid.*, 325 ff.
12. *Sein und Zeit*, 274.
13. *Einführung in die Metaphysik* (Tübingen: Max Niemeyer, 1953), p. 5.
14. *Ibid.*, p. 20.
15. *Was ist Metaphysik?*, 34.
16. *Ibid.*, 51.
17. *Ibid.*, 34.
18. *Ibid.*, 51.
19. *Ibid.*, 35.
20. *Ibid.*, 34.
21. *Ibid.*, 28.
22. *Platons Lehre von der Wahrheit. Mit einem Brief über den Humanismus* (Bern: A. Francke, 1947), p. 113.
23. *Einführung in die Metaphysik*, p. 111. Parmenides' maxim reads: τὸ γὰρ αὐτὸ νοεῖν ἐστίν τε καὶ εἶναι.
24. *Identität und Differenz* (Pfullingen: Neske, 1957), 23 ff.
25. *Einführung in die Metaphysik*, pp. 47-8.
26. *Platons Lehre von der Wahrheit*, p. 32.
27. *Ibid.*
28. *Brief über den Humanism*, p. 53.
29. *Ibid.*, 60.
30. *Was ist Metaphysik?*, 47.
31. *Ibid.*, 10.
32. *Ibid.*, 12.

33. *Brief über den Humanismus,* 66.
34. *Ibid.,* 82.
35. *Gelassenheit* (Pfullingen: Neske, 1959), p. 27.
36. *Ibid.*
37. *Ibid.,* 45.
38. *Ibid.,* 53.
39. *Ibid.,* 44.
40. Cf. Heinrich Ott, *Denken und Sein: Der Weg Martin Heideggers und der Weg der Theologie* (Switzerland: Evangelisches Verlag A. G. Zollikon, 1959); *The Later Heidegger and Theology.* Ed. James M. Robinson and John B. Cobb (New York: Harper & Row, 1963); John Macquarrie, *An Existentialist Theology* (New York: Harper Torchbooks, 1965); also Peter C. Hodgson, "Heidegger, Revelation, and the Word of God," *The Journal of Religion.* 49 (1969), pp. 228-52.

10

MAN SUSPENDED IN MID-AIR: RUDOLF BULTMANN ON THE BELIEVER AS FREE FOR THE FUTURE

Rudolf Bultmann (1884-) understands himself as standing within a long tradition of philosophical and theological reflection. His Biblical studies have been of monumental significance, yet he is modest in evaluating his own crucial contribution to New Testament studies. He asserts that he wishes only to carry Paul's and Luther's doctrine of justification by faith to "its logical conclusion in the field of epistemology." [1] Here as in Luther the dialectic is between faith and unfaith: for both Bultmann and Luther faith becomes a continual conquest of "unfaith." Luther's struggle for faith is still the problem and opportunity for contemporary man, Bultmann holds, but Luther's conception of faith must be updated to make it a live option in the age of telecommunications and space exploration.

Indebtedness to Barth and Heidegger

Bultmann has also acknowledged his indebtedness, and has made his own contributions, to two more recent revolutions, the dialectical theology of Barth and the Barthians and the existential philosophy of Martin Heidegger.[2] He has shared with Barth the opposition to every ontological approach to God; he gladly joined

in the polemic against every historicism and psychologism in theology. He agreed with Barth on the miracle of faith over against all objectification of the act of faith. Barth's existential exegesis of the text of Romans was a production quite congenial to Bultmann. [3] He applauded Barth's dialectic of cleavage between the human and divine, but for himself he has chosen a path of continuity between the two via a concept of existence he owes to Heidegger. Regarding the special significance of existential philosophy for theology he points to its functional priority, "The 'right' philosophy is simply one which has worked out an appropriate terminology for the understanding of existence, an understanding involved in human existence itself." [4] He accepts Heidegger's analysis of man's condition and emphasizes the adequacy of this framework—given the addition of the grace-event—for the presentation of the Christian message today. He considers Heidegger's existential analysis of the essential, formal structures of man's existence adequate both for the life of faith and for unbelief. The faith-decision to seize the original possibilities open to *Dasein* does not alter the structures of *Dasein* or *das Seiende;* it does, according to Bultmann, enable faith to provide an answer to the riddle of *Dasein.* He says of the intimate relationship between believing and unbelieving *Dasein* that, "the structures of *Dasein* presented by philosophy are valid for believing *Dasein* as well." [5] Faith does not alter human nature. Philosophical analysis is not even "completed" or "corrected" by theology.[6] To think otherwise is to misunderstand the nature of faith. Faith can only be understood as, "concrete resolve, as a concrete decision, in a concrete situation constituted by the word of proclamation and by the neighbor. Faith's claim that such a concrete resolve reconstitutes the basic conception of *Dasein,* so that now in addition to an unbelieving *Dasein* there is also a believing *Dasein,* is its specific, its offense." [7] However, Bultmann does not choose to appropriate the material understanding of *Dasein* which Heidegger supplies to these structures or to share Heidegger's philosophical presuppositions, which would conflict with the presuppositions of faith. [8]

Whether he has been able to operate with such a neutral set of structures or whether he has been able to overcome their limitations through his own reading of the Christian faith has been the sub-

ject of extensive debate.[9] However, Heidegger's rejection of all essentialism, all attempts to objectify the person, to reduce the "I" of *Dasein* to *das Seiende,* the subject of everyday and scientific knowledge, seems to Bultmann to offer a view of man with immense potential for theological construction. The concept of existence present here enables him to concentrate on the concrete historical individual rather than on an abstract speculative view of man. It enables him to explore the dialectic of existence, to examine in the light of New Testament insights the distinctive possibilities open to *Dasein.* Thus all Biblical concepts and narratives are interpreted in an existential manner rather than in substantial terms: they depict ways of being, possibilities of human existence. Bultmann sees no difficulty in agreeing with Heidegger that existence is the way of being which discloses possibilities. Existence in the Bible, too, is quest rather than fulfilled reality. Certainly my existence can be no closed phenomenon which I "possess" as I possess knowledge that two and two are four or that the Council of Nicea occurred in 325 A.D.[10] Bultmann sees remarkable analogues to Heidegger everywhere in the New Testament, but particularly in Paul's use of the term σῶμα (body), which points to just such possibilities. There are different dimensions, Paul suggests, in which lives can be lived. Actually the possibilities become dual—either to be at one with the self or to be estranged from one's self. One may lose his grip on his self and come under the control of an alien power, i.e., have a relationship against God, or he can be in control of himself, i.e., be determined by the power of God.[11]

Distinctions from Heidegger

However, Heidegger's failure to come to grips with the problem of God, his enmirement in *das Nichts,* becomes for Bultmann a serious inadequacy to which his own theology provides an answer. His own theistic approach, he holds, offers a more adequate answer to the question of human existence in responsibility and freedom than Heidegger's non-theistic approach via *Sein* (Being). In faith's readiness to face dread not only is the facticity of man's existence disclosed to him but the possibility of God also appears. In other words, one is freed through faith from himself (his old

self) for himself (his new self).[12] To speak of an act of God simply means to speak of one's self as being existentially concerned.[13] There is no possibility, for Bultmann, to speak of God as some metaphysical, given reality. God is no cosmic thing. He says, "His Being (existence) is understood aright only when it is understood as significant-for-man being . . ."[14] A whole world separates theoretical understanding, or theoretical "proof" of God's existence, from existential understanding. God—or the activity of God—is visible only to faith. There is also no possibility to speak of God in a static, undialectical manner because of the disproportion between man's speech and the divine speech.[15] And there is no way to an understanding of the mysteries of life and death, sin and grace, apart from resolve and decision.[16]

But again in distinction from Heidegger, it is not man's nature itself but the word of the gospel that leads to a new understanding of the self. The return to man's origins is possible for Bultmann only through the challenge to a new openness which the proclamation of the gospel brings. Bultmann couples his concentration on a new self-understanding with concern for what occurs in preaching. Preaching declares this unique Christian message of the grace of God always personally and individually, not as some general truth addressed to everyone, but as a word from another person addressed "to you and to me."[17] And it is repentance and faith rather than an act of resolve *(Entschlossenheit)* and "patient noble-mindedness" that opens man's possibilities to himself.[18]

Heidegger's basic opposition between inauthentic and authentic self is given a theological interpretation by Bultmann in terms of sin and grace. In his exposition of Paul's theology these basic possibilities appear as living according to the "flesh" (*σάρξ*) or according to the "spirit" (*πνεῦμα*). One can rely on his own strength, may pursue his own creaturely desires, and so be at war with himself, or he can trust in the gift of grace, can live in openness to the future, i.e., he may choose to live for God. Thus man can either lose his self or he can win it. In John's theology it is the possibility of existing under God's wrathful judgment in a perverted *cosmos* or of deciding against the world and for God.[19] Through faith the believer lives an unworldly existence already now within the world.

Thus Bultmann is interested no less than Heidegger in the "true existence" of man over against a "lost existence." In this relationship between inauthentic and authentic Bultmann appropriates the dialectic of Luther in asserting that, "the justified one is justified only in his relation to God and always only in relation to God and is upon earth a sinner." [20] Man is to be seen as losing his true self in his escape from personal responsibility. He lives a life of care ending in death. But he is also to be understood in terms of his call before God to a radical new obedience. Jesus Christ is God's gracious offer of a new way—in Bultmann's terms, of a new understanding of the self. Thus Bultmann correlates the ways of being in existential philosophy with key Biblical concepts.

The Meaning of History

No less significant is Bultmann's view of history. All of history is focused upon the decisive end-event, Jesus Christ as end of the old existence. Jesus opened a new possibility to man in his fallenness. He proclaimed the possibility, in radical openness to what the future offers, to receive no less than a new self by the grace of God. Jesus himself is God's eschatological event by which he has set an end to the present course of the world: the rule of Satan and all the Satanic powers is drawing to its close; God's reign is even now, and ever and again dawning. [21] The entire course of universal history is focused upon the individual in the present moment. This moment is big, for one who enters into this eschatological Christ-event, with the same eschatological possibilities. The present is the moment of decision. [22] The historical Jesus represents this call to radical decision. He himself signified this challenge to decision. [23] Men must be ready to renounce this world's goods and attendant cares in favor of radical obedience to God's will for them. [24] No facet of man's knowing and willing and doing was to be left untouched by this altered understanding of the self. An entirely new vista is gained upon one's world, upon one's neighbor, and upon one's own past and future. [25] The "obedience of faith" Bultmann sees as no human accomplishment or "work;" it represents a most intimate fusion of doer and deed. [26]

The existential framework is always decisive, as when Bult-

mann says of faith that it "realizes itself in concrete living: in the individual acts of the man of faith." [27] Existence is realized by personal decision in concrete encounters in the flow of specific occasions. This faith is no secure possession, no settled condition. In the decision of faith man chooses the possibilities to live from the power of God again and again. Ever and again he slips back from his real historical existence into bondage to this present world, to the tyranny the New Testament connects with a fallen *cosmos*. Ever and again he projects himself, he must choose his own distinct possibilities. His essence is nothing other than the sum total of decisions he has made in the past. As existing *(ex-sistere)* man stands out from the being of things; he is not something fixed, he is never complete; he chooses, through his decisions, who he is to become.

The Dialectic of Freedom

Bultmann finds this dialectic of Christian existence clearly and coherently expressed in St. Paul. It is the dialectic of slavery and freedom. "For freedom," Bultmann says, "is nothing else than being open for the genuine future, letting one's self be determined by the future." [28] Man is enslaved to the desires of this present world, to guilt, and death. He is bound in care to perishable things. In Pauline terms, natural man stands in slavish obedience to the law; he is far removed from that radical obedience to God's will which Paul connects with faith. He is, in fact, agitated by the most contradictory influences and emotions. Yet his inner freedom counteracts such turbulence with the great Pauline ὡς μή (as though):

> From now on, let those who have wives live
> as though they had none,
> And those who mourn
> as though they were not mourning,
> And those who rejoice
> as though they were not rejoicing,
> And those who buy
> as though they had no goods,
> And those who deal with the world,
> as though they had no dealings with it.
> (I Cor. 7:29-31)

Through the word of preaching men are summoned out of their fallen existence and are challenged to decision, i.e., they are confronted with their authentic possibility. The eschatological Christ-event repeatedly becomes present to faith through preaching.[29] So Bultmann sees Christ's death and resurrection as a unitary salvation-occurrence constantly recurring in the "now" of preaching: "the salvation-occurrence is nowhere present except in the proclaiming, accosting, demanding, and promising word of preaching."[30] In other words, this existence of faith can be seen as a dialectic of being on the way, between "no longer" and "not yet:" "The decision of faith has done away with the past; nevertheless, as true decision, the decision must be maintained—that is, made again and again anew. As that which is overcome, the past is always with us, and faith must remember the past as that which constantly threatens."[31] What is important here is the dialectic of present possession and future fulfillment, "The believer must still become what he already is, and is already what he shall become. He is in the freedom into which he is brought by his faith, and which shows itself by obedience."[32]

This makes of the man of faith a person suspended in mid-air.[33] He has left the presumed *terra firma* of proofs and demonstrations and securities. Nor can he clutch for assurances in "works" or in any Biblical authority. Nothing terrestrial or superterrestrial appears to support him. Faith involves this impossible feat— impossible except for the dialectic of concrete decision.

Notes

1. *Kerygma and Myth,* ed. Hans Werner Bartsch (New York: Harper Torchbooks, 1961), p. 211.
2. Cf. "Autobiographical Reflections of Rudolf Bultmann," *The Theology of Rudolf Bultmann,* ed. Charles W. Kegley (New York: Harper & Row, 1966), pp. xxiii-xxiv.
3. R. Bultmann, "Karl Barths 'Römerbrief' in zweiter Auflage," *Christliche Welt,* 36. Jg. 1922. Reprinted in *Anfänge der dialektischen Theologie.* Hsgn. Jürgen Moltmann (München: Chr. Kaiser Verlag, 1966). Teil I, p. 119 ff.
4. *Kerygma and Myth,* 193.
5. R. Bultmann, "Das Problem der natürlichen Theologie," *Glauben und*

Verstehen (Tübingen: J. C. B. Mohr, 1954), I, p. 308. Translated by Louise Pettibone Smith as *Faith and Understanding* (New York: Harper and Row, 1969).

6. *Ibid.*, 309.
7. Ibid., 310.
8. Otto Schnübbe, *Der Existenzbegriff in der Theologie Rudolf Bultmanns* (Göttingen: Vandenhoeck & Ruprecht, 1959). p. 25.
9. Cf. the discussion and literature cited in Schnübbe, *op. cit.*, p. 34 ff.
10. R. Bultmann, "Die Bedeutung der 'dialektischen Theologie' für die neutestamentliche Wissenschaft," *Glauben und Verstehen,* I, p. 121.
11. R. Bultmann, *Theology of the New Testament.* Tr. Kendrick Grobel (London: S.C.M. Press, 1952) I, 196 ff.
12. *Kerygma and Myth,* 205-6.
13. *Ibid.*, 196 ff. Cf. also "Welchen Sinn hat es, von Gott zu reden?" *Glauben und Verstehen,* I, pp. 26-37.
14. *Theology of the New Testament,* I, 229.
15. R. Bultmann, "Die Frage der 'dialektischen' Theologie," reprinted from *Zwischen den Zeiten,* 4 Jg. 1926, Heft 1, S. 40-59, in *Anfänge der dialektischen Theologie,* II, p. 79.
16. *Glauben und Verstehen,* I, 127.
17. R. Bultmann, *The Presence of Eternity* (New York: Harper & Brothers, 1957), p. 151.
18. Cf. Heidegger, *Discourse on Thinking,* 85.
19. *Theology of the New Testament,* II, 76.
20. *Glauben und Verstehen,* I, 311.
21. *The Presence of Eternity,* 141.
22. *Ibid.*
23. *Theology of the New Testament,* I, 9.
24. *Ibid.*, 10 f.
25. *Kerygma and Myth,* 203.
26. *Theology of the New Testament,* I, 316.
27. *Ibid.*, p. 324.
28. *Ibid.*, 335.
29. *The Presence of Eternity,* p. 151.
30. *Theology of the New Testament,* I, 302.
31. *Ibid.*, 322.
32. *The Presence of Eternity,* 48.
33. *Kerygma and Myth,* 211.

11

STRUGGLER UNDER THE TWOFOLD VERDICT OF GOD:

WERNER ELERT AND THE DIALECTIC OF LAW AND GOSPEL

The issue of the proper relationship between law and gospel has always been with the Church. Already at the core of the Old Testament understanding of man are the themes of sin and grace. When Paul asserts, Romans 10:3, that "Christ is the end of the law" he is not relaxing the tension he otherwise emphasizes between life as task and as gift. He rather raises with new urgency the role of the law for the Christian. A great deal of confusion has been introduced where Luther's dialectic of law and gospel has been superimposed on New Testament texts without due attention to the historical situation from which both Luther and the Biblical writers speak. Following Luther's decisive confrontation with the question of man's righteousness before God, a new urgency, an urgency still present, was given the entire question of the proper relation between law and gospel. No one has fought more vigorously to defend a dialectical relationship between them than Werner Elert (1885-1954). For Elert the entire dynamic of divine-human relationships—and of the divine activity itself—requires that one recognize this dialectic at the center of Christian theology.

In the seminal sources of law and gospel he finds the contradictory contents of God's revelation.

Barth's False Dialectic

The law is revealed for a distinctive function, to work retribution. Thus it prepares in a strictly dialectical manner for the revelation of grace through the gospel. Here, Elert insists, is to be found the real dialectic of the Christian faith in contrast to the apparent dialectic between God and man, between divine revelation and human endeavors which Karl Barth attempted to reassert. Elert says of Barth's dialectic, "Here the essential matter of revelation is not taken seriously, not *what* God speaks, but *that* God speaks, not what man hears, but that he hears." [1] A decisive shift from the basic distinction between law and gospel, wrath and grace, came with the subordination of this valid concern for the *material* content of Reformation theology to the false concern for the *form* of revelation, thus becoming the question of the relationship between reason and revelation. [2] The concern of theology came to be true versus false revelation, with "natural revelation," with the revelation of God as he is "in and for himself," rather than with revelation as it always occurs in its concrete, twofold manifestation in law and gospel. As a reflection of this concern in Karl Barth, Elert points out that not a trace of reference to the law appears in the Barmen Declaration. [3] He says of law and gospel in Barth, "According to Barth, they describe only one and the same act of God, which in its *content* is always the same and merely manifests itself in two different ways of speaking. When God speaks the law, then, that is always at the same time promise, *therefore* also gospel. When, on the other hand, he speaks in the gospel, then his demanding will speaks there at the same time, therefore the gospel." [4] But Elert distinguishes between two quite different promises here, on the part of the law a promise of grace to the righteous who have fulfilled it, in the case of the gospel a promise of grace to sinners who have failed to fulfill it. What is *promised* in law and in gospel is applied to radically different recipients: i.e., the quality of their life before God cannot be left out of account.

Wrath and Grace

Within God himself Elert points to a dialectic of wrath and grace, corresponding to the dual foci of law and gospel in his revelations. He points to the linking of wrath and law in Romans 4:15, "For the law brings wrath, but where there is no law there is no transgression." [5] Another dialectic with regard to man corresponds to these, the dialectic of sin and faith. [6] For as man's sin gives rise to God's wrath so is his righteousness bestowed upon faith by means of the gospel, "For in it the righteousness of God is revealed through faith for faith" (Rom 1:17). Man always stands under the judgment of God. This judgment, however, entails one verdict according to its examination of the quality of man's life under the law (the quality Elert explores in his ethics under the category of "nomological existence") and another verdict as it reflects the pronouncement of forgiveness under the gospel (the quality described as "Ethos under Grace").[7] This twofold judgment often appears as a dualism, reminiscent of Luther's *"duo tot homines."* However, by reason of the transition from unjust to just and vice versa this dual judgment becomes a highly dialectical notion in Elert.

Man's nomological existence under God's law represents a total ordering of social and biological, natural and historical processes. This ordering forms a bulwark against chaos. *Nomos* controls blind chance and arbitrariness and as such provides man with much-needed security. But these same laws that furnish security also finally work one's death and dissolution. The law is a vast system of rewards and punishments.[8] It requires of man that he justify the totality of his existence before God. But it becomes painfully evident that man stands in sinful contradiction over against God rather than in pleasant harmony with the divine will.

Christian theology and ethics must be crystal-clear as to whether they speak of the judgment of God under the law or under the gospel. Under God's verdict of the law man stands condemned. He is guilty and a sinner. This verdict is always negative, i.e., *Lex semper accusat.* It is a hypocritical misunderstanding of the divine judgment inherent in the law's demands if one supposes he is living in full conformity to these demands. All men without

exception stand under the law of God. [9] As a correlate to the law's demand, both believer and unbeliever are confronted with the just wrath of God visited on all unrighteousness. The unbeliever is, whether he recognizes it or not, under the devastating anger of God; he is subject to the curse of God's disapproval, and is under sentence of eternal death. The believer does not cease to stand under this judgment of condemnation, since the law's uncompromising demands still make their claims on him. But by virtue of his trust in the Word of forgiveness the word of wrath has become God's penultimate word for him. He is sinner, indeed, and this word continues to be a valid word on the quality of his life, but another Word, that of gospel, pronounces him a sinner forgiven.

It should be noted that Elert finds the emphasis of the New Testament not on God's wrath to come, at the end of this present age, but on the present visitation of divine anger on all lawlessness: "*Now* is the wrath of God being revealed on all unrighteousness." (Romans 1:18). He does not deny that New Testament usage has a place for the eschatological irruption of wrath, but man now and continually stands under the implacable, death-dealing judgment of condemnation. God is thus seen not from an ontological or mystical framework but from a moral perspective, i.e., in a framework of law, as functioning through his law to judge, to oppose, to condemn, and destroy all evil—including the considerable evil remaining in the regenerate. Forgiveness is no matter-of-course affair but requires continual repentance for offenses against God's law—the negation of sin—and faith in Christ—the affirmation of grace. The believer must be told that he continues to sin much—and thereby the law continues to negate the word of the gospel, which announces to man the removal of sin. This action is twofold: it is because the law continually convicts of sin that we must steadfastly reaffirm our faith, or as Elert states the dialectic, "precisely the gospel establishes the validity of the law—the same law the validity of which is "overcome" by the gospel." [10]

God's Twofold Verdicts on Man

God's verdict on the man who trusts the gospel reflects the reality of divine forgiveness and is thus a verdict of "not guilty."

The believer stands simultaneously under the two-fold judgment of God, under that of his law, which finds him a sinner, and the gospel, which declares him forgiven *propter Christum.* He stands simultaneously under wrath and grace, the *"favor dei."* It is the encounter with Christ that intervenes to alter the decisive judgment of God. As the sinless one who is yet the friend of sinners he elevates sinners into equality with him and wipes out the difference between them.[11] A "harmony of opposites" occurs in the presence of the Christ at table with the sinner where the "joyful exchange" takes place. A new quality is imparted to human ethos by God's announcement of forgiveness.

Elert traces this dialectic to the oppositions in St. Paul's letters, in the Gospels, and in the account of Abraham's sacrifice of Isaac. It is the "infinite resignation" of Abraham, by which he renounces the finite for the sake of the infinite, that characterizes the Christian faith. In the beatitudes all earthly goods—health, food, and comfort—are renounced until they are restored by faith. The believer is in the dialectical situation of "having nothing" and "yet possessing all things" (II Cor. 6:10). In the wording of the beatitudes even the "earth" will be restored to them (Matt. 5:5). However, the man of faith, simply because he faces the challenge to act either in faith or lack of faith experiences the anguish of a continual, invisible struggle. He pits himself against formidable odds, "When he believes, however, he believes against the law, against condemnation, against fate, against contradiction. Even more: he believes against the God of the law and condemnation because he believes in *that* God who is revealed and calls for reconciliation in his Son." [12]

Under the law he stands condemned, yet under the gospel he is pardoned. In this divergence the ground of the dialectic is to be found. The inner nature of the law is that it entails retribution. God promises grace and every blessing on all who keep his commandments, on those, then, who actually succeed in keeping the law, but he threatens with punishment all who transgress the commandments. Luther's summary of the commandments as promise and threat is seen as a classic statement of retribution in the Decalogue.[13] On the other hand, the exclusiveness of the dialectic is expressed in the formula: "Where the voice of the law

is heard the voice of the gospel is silent. Where the voice of the gospel is heard the voice of the law is silent." [14] Here Elert emphasizes the contradictions in these twofold "words" of God, between revelation in one "word" and a corresponding veiling of the other. But just as little as these opposites are confused in God's revealing and veiling so little should they be confused in man's understanding and proclamation. Law and gospel are genuine "contradictions" of God. In speaking his word of grace in the gospel God saves from his own threat of punishment in the law: one word of God encounters and opposes the other.[15]

Elert's cardinal opposition is directed against any and all efforts to break this dialectic by reinterpreting the gospel as law or by deriving the law from the gospel, as Karl Barth does. He attacks all efforts to resolve the conflicting phenomena of law and gospel, or, what amounts to the same thing, to escape the verdicts with which all genuine theology is concerned, the twofold verdicts of condemnation and grace. In every effort to evade these distinct verdicts, as, e.g., in "overcoming" the opposition through some unifying concept such as the "word of God," he sees a betrayal which results in subverting both law and gospel: the law is deprived of its convicting power, and the gospel is robbed of its saving power, i.e., the death of Christ is finally made of no effect because the law is not recognized in all its death-dealing significance. Only in Christ is the conflict between God's word and judgment as law and his word and judgment as gospel reconciled.

The Uses of the Law

The opposition becomes clear when one evaluates the law properly in its primary function of convicting of sin. Elert appeals to Luther's understanding of the twofold use of the law *(duplex usus legis)*. The proper use of the law *(usus proprius,* i.e., *theologicus* or *spiritualis)* is to reveal to men that they are sinners before God. This above all must be seen as the real functioning of the law; it must be acknowledged as incapable of fulfillment. Man recognizes himself as undone before the law's inveterate demands, because the law is not merely a body of divine legislation but is God's active administration of justice, God's judicatory function

(Judikatur Gottes).[16] Melanchthon's dictum spells this out uncompromisingly, "the law always accuses," *"Lex semper accusat."* [17] When properly understood the law cannot function as it did for Calvin as a rule of living, as *"reigle de bien vivre et justement."* [18] Through the law God is always active *judging* man. Calvin's misunderstanding was to see the law exclusively as the expression of God's legislative action instead of seeing it more radically and more essentially as always judgmental in character.[19] And when this judgmental character is seen properly it is seen as accusing man, more properly as condemning him to death. The law condemns man as Christ himself was condemned to death and suffered death by the law.

Following Luther, Elert also points to a second use of the law, a social function *(usus politicus* or *usus civilis),* according to which evil is held externally in check, so that the earthly life of mankind is not completely destroyed.[20] But in every effort to establish a third use of the law *(tertius usus legis)* Elert sees an attempt to mediate the *"Realdialektik"* of law and gospel, thus a solemn betrayal of both the law and the gospel. Faith is always bound up with repentance: one must first be convicted of sin and have a heartfelt desire for release from God's just penalties before faith in Christ's work can avail. The third use is ostensibly to inform the regenerate *(usus didacticus).*[21] But Elert contends that Luther knew nothing of such an "informational" or "disciplinary" use for the regenerate. He knew of no "Christian ethics," i.e., an ethic which sets forth the norms by which the believer should guide his everyday life, in contrast to his theological ethics, which is inextricably bound to faith in the gospel. The regenerate man, insofar as he is renewed, i.e., under the guidance and power of the Holy Spirit, has no need for law. The law has no dominion over him. One has no protection, however, simply because one is a Christian, against the threats of punishment in the law. The old Adam continues to assert itself, and the flesh continues to war against the spirit in the regenerate. The law is necessary not for the new man but precisely because of self-assertion of the old man.[22]

It was Melanchthon, Elert holds, who developed such an inconsistent use within Lutheranism. Melanchthon took this step in order to meet the threat of libertinism on the part of the en-

thusiasts. Yet he retained this key agreement with Luther, both saw in the judgmental function of the law the *praecipuus usus*.[23] Calvin in his *Institutes* of 1539 and following editions accorded this informational use the role of *praecipuus* and *proprius*.[24] The law in its essential nature is rule of life rather than God's judgment on man. The goal of God's entire legislative activity became for Calvin precisely this full obedience to the law which is embraced in his conception of the *tertius usus legis*. So the gospel does not offer a new way of salvation but merely clarifies what is already present in the law.[25] Its function becomes quite incidental, then, to the overriding function of the law, "The gospel clears away all the difficulties that prevent its being kept." [26]

Irreconcilable Divergence

At each step Elert emphasizes divergence rather than continuity between law and gospel. Retribution is quite a different thing from grace. The gospel introduces a radical new way of salvation, also a way of life different from the way of the law, a kairological sense of time in contrast to chronological existence, a kingdom of grace distinct from God's rule by law in his earthly kingdom. Within the Christian fellowship it is quite another ordering that prevails in place of the coercion common to all political order. The Christian brotherhood is ordered by "the law of Christ" (Gal. 6:2).[27] Failure to recognize the difference here has resulted in mistaking this brotherhood, too, as a political, or quasi-political entity—an error for which the Calvinist tradition has consistently exhibited a marked proclivity. But Elert holds that the new creation stemming from the work of Christ is powered not by a measured or commanded love which is the highest attainment in the political sphere but by a love that extends even to one's enemy, which is ready, like the love of Christ, to be betrayed.[28] Such a love cannot be expected of any political power. The most one can and should expect in this realm is the law of retribution. Here the rule of distributive justice, the Ciceronian "*suum cuique tribuens*," "to give each his own," becomes the norm and even the supreme achievement of political justice. Elert traces the New Testament distinctions between the two realms, the two ways, and the two kinds of

time to what he describes as the "objectively irreconcilable divergence" of law and gospel.[29] Were it not for the presence of faith in the gospel—and the continual challenge to live by this faith—there would be no conflict with the claims of the earthly realm, with the wide road, or with chronological time. In each of these categories the decisive struggle is between faith and unfaith, or, what is the same thing, between the new self and the old. Justification does not establish some kind of "stability of being." [30] The new self affirms itself over against the old self "from circumstance to circumstance, from act to act." [31]

If one looks for a resolution of the "address" and "counter-address" of faith and unfaith, law and gospel in Elert then he directs one to a sole person, Jesus Christ. The voice of the law is silenced through God's own action in Christ: "He alone can silence it, because he in contrast to all others completely fulfilled and fully suffered the law's demands." [32] By bearing in his own body the penalty for the guilt of all mankind he invalidated the claims of law—i.e., law's demands and gospel grace converge here—and only here.[33] Faith, therefore, by attaching itself to this crucified and risen Jesus, becomes man's sole resource for overcoming the contradictions of law and gospel. The gospel is, like the law, also "word" from God, a self-manifestation of God, but the content of this word is a person, Christ.[34] This is the Christ of the saving word and works, the Christ who came "not to destroy the law, but to fulfill it," i.e., to be the fulfillment of all prophecy.[35] This is the Christ who in the New Testament is set over against God's wrath, the one who freely and sinlessly sustained in his death on the cross God's just retribution upon the entire nomological existence of mankind.[36] In his resurrection God accepts the reconciling death of Jesus and thus puts an end to nomological existence and institutes a new order of existence. This is the Jesus who proclaimed the continuing validity of the law's requirements more uncompromisingly than did the scribes and Pharisees. He uncovered the secret sins of the heart—in which evil thoughts and desires lurk. To be sure, he proclaimed the supremacy of love for God and the neighbor, but he was specific in pointing out that the law of love found men wanting.

Among Sticky Wickets

The dialectic of law and gospel in Elert is an impressive and incisive instrument for the interpretation of Scripture—and, indeed, of the human condition. One must agree with Luther that for the understanding of Scripture and all of theology everything depends on the proper distinction between law and gospel. Still one senses that both the variety of the concrete Biblical narrative and the constructive ends of God's working in history are not adequately handled by these contradictions. The split phases of law and gospel must be seen in more adequate relationship to certain other fundamental themes of the New Testament. In fact, we propose that it is precisely the reality of God that is lost in favor of these divine activities. Man's relation to the *deus loquens* in Luther's thought becomes in Elert a relationship to the law, to certain abstract principles of divine truth.

Certainly the concept of *nomos* in Old and New Testament is a complex one, with aspects to which Elert devotes little attention. For Paul it is primarily the Torah of Moses given 430 years after the promise (Gal. 3, 17). For Judaism today, too, law is essentially Torah, read, however, as described in the Psalms, as gracious gift from God. It is an expression of God's favor for his people, a channel of his lovingkindness. Elert severs law and gospel from their historical matrix in an abstract emphasis on contradiction. God's righteousness in its Biblical framework is more dynamic, personal, and constructive in its ends than Elert allows. Salvation and fulfillment are the ends to be served by the destructive wrath of God against all that resists love. Elert has illumined the condition of man by his concentration on this form of dialectic, but at the price of that purpose which imparts meaning to all the ways of God. An examination of the Biblical concept of repentance would point to this goal-directed character of God's working in law and gospel. God destroys what is opposed to him in order that he may impart his light and life. He establishes his covenant with his people as a people united under the divine law, so that covenant and "holy nation" provide the framework for social legislation and God's judgment. Elert's system of complementary divine verdicts has the advantage of refusing to reduce

the divine activity to some simple rational harmony. Still one finds the Biblical perspective on the dynamic coherence of all of life strangely lacking here.

Notes

1. Werner Elert, "Gesetz und Evangelium," *Zwischen Gnade und Ungnade: Abwandlungen des Themas Gesetz und Evangelium* (München: Evangelischer Presseverband, 1948), p. 133. Tr. by Edward H. Schroeder as *Law and Gospel* (Philadelphia: Fortress Press, 1967).
2. Elert sees the decisive step within Lutheranism being taken here by Melanchthon, cf. *Die Morphologie des Luthertums* (München: C. H. Beck'sche Verlagsbuchhandlung, 1931), I, 46 ff.
3. *Zwischen Gnade und Ungnade,* p. 134.
4. *Ibid.,* p. 135.
5. Werner Elert, *Der christliche Glaube: Grundlinien der lutherischen Dogmatik* (Hamburg: Furche-Verlag, dritte, ergänzte Auflage, 1956), p. 139.
6. *Ibid.*
7. Werner Elert, *Das christliche Ethos: Grundlinien der lutherischen Ethik* Tübingen: Furche-Verlag, 1949). Tr. as *The Christian Ethos* (Philadelphia: Muhlenberg, 1957). *Passim.*
8. *The Christian Ethos,* 52.
9. *Ibid., Der christliche Glaube.*
10. *Der christliche Glaube,* 140.
11. *The Christian Ethos,* 177 ff.
12. *Der christliche Glaube,* 285.
13. Werner Elert, "The Third Use of the Law," *The Lutheran World Review,* vol. I, no. 3 (January, 1949), p. 42.
14. *Zwischen Gnade und Ungnade,* 132.
15. *Der christliche Glaube,* 141.
16. *Zwischen Gnade und Ungnade,* 138.
17. *Ibid.,* quoting from the Apology of the Augsburg Confession, IV, *de just.,* 167.
18. *Ibid.,* quoting from Article Three of the Geneva Catechism of 1536; 136.
19. "The Third Use of the Law," 41.
20. *Zwischen Gnade und Ungnade,* 143.
21. Cf. *ibid.,* 161 ff., also *The Christian Ethos,* 294 ff.
22. *The Christian Ethos,* 297.
23. *Ibid.,* 300-09.
24. "The Third Use of the Law," 41
25. *Ibid.*
26. *Ibid.,* 44.
27. *Ibid.,* 45.
28. *Ibid.*

29. *The Christian Ethos*, 283 ff.
30. *Der christliche Glaube*, 488.
31. *Ibid.*
32. *Ibid.*, 143.
33. *Ibid.*, 142.
34. *Zwischen Gnade und Ungnade*, 144.
35. *Ibid.*, 145, quoting Matt. 5:17.
36. *The Christian Ethos*, 188 ff.

EPILOG

It has been the peculiar task of theology in the modern world to learn to think dialectically, since it can no longer presuppose the correlation between the human and divine, the natural and the supernatural, of more unified world-views. Each of the Lutheran representatives in the chapters preceding reveals the extent to which the "dark side of life" impinges upon man's personal consciousness. Always the reaches of indescribable suffering and joy present themselves. There is a refusal to reduce the mighty opposites which present themselves to human experience into a rational system. Here Luther's *Urerlebnis* of the togetherness of an earthly and heavenly reality in the experience of justification became decisive in setting a certain pattern. Moreover, each of the theologians represented here presents a commentary on Luther's dictum that God in his revelation is always hidden *sub contraria specie.* Even Heidegger's elusive Being uncovers itself by way of *das Nichts.*

The truth in dialectic is the truth of disciplined discourse—between man and man, or between man and God. Plato already employed insights here which are startling in their simplicity, yet explosive in their implications. Thinking itself is dialogue. It is asking questions and giving answers. It is saying Yes or No—

or perhaps both. The logos demands such a dialogical approach to establish its truth. This is the original and basic form of dialectical thinking, even though we have noted an infinite variety of specific operations in the discourses of our pre-eminent dialecticians. Dialectic is nothing foreign to thinking; rather where serious thinking is engaged in there dialectic, the examination of contradiction, is inescapable. The opponents of dialectic in this sense—and Plato indicates they are many, coming in many stripes—are simply opposed to any genuine quest for truth, for even divine truth must be expressed in the earthen vessels of human words. Each of our dialecticians has emphasized the need for a stricter discipline in discourse. They have pointed to contradictions and uncovered identities which have illuminated the human condition.

It is impossible to reduce the forms of dialectic presented in the preceding chapters to some least common denominator which is the technique of dialectical unfolding. The form taken corresponds in each instance to the nature of the oppositions, the reconciling principles, and the goal of final synthesis. Each consistent dialectic seeks, finally, to overcome the contradictions in reality or thinking or doing, and by transcending the incongruities of life to arrive at an inclusive unity, as Hegel, for example, reconciles the contradictions in reality as stages in the unfolding of Absolute Spirit. Even Kierkegaard anticipates such a "higher," future synthesis, though each sphere of existence will continue to face heightened contradictions.

It is clear that two major types of dialectic appear, one which emphasizes opposition or contradiction—Luther, Pascal, Kierkegaard, Barth, Elert—and the other which terminates in mediation or reconciliation—Boehme, Hegel, and Tillich, and probably also Heidegger and Bultmann. The first appears to be more "static," since it does not drive forward, like the dynamic second type, to resolution in a third, unifying principle. Yet as avowedly Christian theologians—with the exception of Heidegger—each of the forms of dialectic examined finds its resolution, in one shape or another, in a doctrine of Christ. St. Paul's Christology set a pattern for this when he observed that "in him all things hold together." Cusanus was to find in Christ the reconciliation of all contraries. Kierkegaard answers the radical split between God and man with an

equally radical reconciliation in the God-man. Bultmann presents the *crux Christi:* as the call to continually new choice between contradictory ways of being. For Elert it is found in the death and resurrection of Jesus, who in his death bore the full force of the divine wrath and in the resurrection witnesses to the divine gift of grace. Hegel reconciles transcendence and immanence by means of a Trinitarian scheme in which the Second Person opens the way to the plenitude of the Third Person. The dialectics of antithesis and of synthesis both end in reconciliation.

What is important to note, however, is that in each representative the peculiar nature of the oppositions found in reality provides the setting for their reconciliation in the mediating principle. When the mediating principle is found in Christology the oppositions determine the shape of the respective interpretation of Christ. For example, Barth's antithesis between the divine and the human is reconciled in his distinctive "God with us." Tillich's dialectic of essential unity and existential estrangement is reconciled in his "restorative principle," the New Being. So it is not enough to say that the contradictions are finally "resolved" in Christ. One must note that the person and work of Christ function quite differently in each instance—always in relation to the oppositions to be reconciled and the goal of the final synthesis.

What we have found in the course of dialectical "nay-saying" is an illumination of the human condition. Plato's dialectical investigations emerged not so much in a theory of justice or courage or being as in a new self-understanding on the part of the participant. Pascal's analysis of man's disproportion resulted in opening new ranges of self-fulfillment. Hegel's unfolding of Spirit, specious as it is, is most intriguing as it casts light on his central problem—the freedom of the concrete individual. The same can be said, in fact, for each of the representatives we have studied. Plato saw his new self-understanding as no disparagement of his inquiry, nor would any of the dialecticians we have considered. No unilateral view of man can do justice to the many-sided truth of his condition.

Dialectic enables man to see himself as a unity of complementary opposites. Through his awareness of his self as such a unity of opposites man is able to extend the ranges of his possibilities. He

is able to venture beyond himself. He transcends old limits to the self, and by "reaching beyond" into what he was not he realizes his distinctive nature as man. This is what the world's most creative artists did—Goethe in literature, Bach in music, and Michelangelo in art. This is what each of our dialecticians has done with regard to the limits of the soul.

The person becomes the focus of each dialectic—and only dialectic appears to do faint justice to the ranges or "stages," if we wish, of the human soul. The individual takes the contradictions of existence into the mediating fullness of acceptance and decision to emerge fulfilled and cleansed and enriched.

SELECTED BIBLIOGRAPHY

Adler, Mortimer J., *Dialectic*. New York: Harcourt, Brace & Co., 1927.

Barth, Karl, *Christ and Adam. Man and Humanity in Romans 5*. Trans. T. A. Smail. New York: Collier Books, 1962.

Dupre, Louis, *Kierkegaard as Theologian. The Dialectic of Christian Existence.* New York: Sheed and Ward.

Foulquié, Paul, *La Dialectique*. Paris: Presses Universitaires, 1953.

Freeman, Kathleen, *Ancilla to the Pre-Socratic Philosophers,* Cambridge, Mass.: Harvard University Press, 1957.

Guardini, Romano, *Pascal for Our Time*. Trans. Brian Thompson. New York: Herder and Herder, 1966; original edition, 1962.

Hartmann, E. v., *Über die dialektische Methode*. Berlin: Carl Dunker's Verlag, 1868.

Heiss, Robert, *Die grossen Dialektiker des 19. Jahrhunderts*. Berlin: Kiepenhever & Witsch, 1963.

Lee, H. D. P., *Zeno of Elea*. Cambridge: The University Press, 1936.

Moltmann, J., *Anfänge der dialektischen Theologie*. 2 vols. München: Chr. Kaiser Verlag, 1966.

Robinson, Richard, *Plato's Earlier Dialectic*. Second edition. Oxford: The Clarendon Press, 1953.

Sinaiko, Herman L., *Love, Knowledge, and Discourse in Plato*. Chicago: Univ. of Chicago Press, 1965.

Tillich, Paul, *The Interpretation of History*. Trans. N. A. Razetzki and Elsa L. Talmey. New York: Charles Scribner's Sons, 1936.

von Balthasar, Hans Urs, *Karl Barth, Darstellung und Deutung seiner Theologie.* Köln: Jacob Hegner, 2nd. ed., 1962.